T0114305

MANAGING
PEOPLE

... what's personality got to do with it?

<u>Also by Carol Ritberger, Ph.D.</u>

Books

LOVE . . . WHAT'S PERSONALITY GOT TO DO WITH IT?:
Working at Love to Make Love Work

WHAT COLOR IS YOUR PERSONALITY?:
Red, Orange, Yellow, Green . . .

YOUR PERSONALITY, YOUR HEALTH:
Connecting Personality with the Human Energy System,
Chakras, and Wellness

Audio Program (includes workbook)

YOUR PERSONALITY, YOUR HEALTH, AND YOUR LIFE

※ ※ ※

All of the above are available at your local bookstore,
or may be ordered by visiting:

Hay House USA: **www.hayhouse.com**®
Hay House Australia: **www.hayhouse.com.au**
Hay House UK: **www.hayhouse.co.uk**
Hay House India: **www.hayhouseindia.co.in**

MANAGING
PEOPLE

. . . what's personality got to do with it?

CAROL RITBERGER, Ph.D.

HAY HOUSE, INC.
Carlsbad, California
London • Sydney • New Delhi

Published in the United States by: Hay House, Inc.: www.hayhouse.com
Published in Australia by: Hay House Australia Pty. Ltd.: www.hayhouse.com.au
Published in the United Kingdom by: Hay House UK, Ltd.: www.hayhouse.co.uk
Published in India by: Hay House Publishers India: www.hayhouseindia.co.in

Editorial supervision: Jill Kramer • *Design:* Tricia Breidenthal

Library of Congress Cataloging-in-Publication Data

Ritberger, Carol.
  Managing people-- : what's personality got to do with it? / Carol Ritberger. --
1st ed.
      p. cm.
  ISBN-13: 978-1-4019-1034-1 (tradepaper) 1. Personnel management. 2. Interpersonal relations. 3. Typology (Psychology) I. Title.
  HF5549.R537 2007
  658.3--dc22

                                        2006028654

ISBN: 978-1-4019-1034-1

1st edition, April 2007
1st digital printing, January 2016

Printed in the United States of America

To my daughter, Diana.

*The art of management is to accomplish
desired objectives through the contributions of
others. Your skill and ability to achieve exceptional
results by enabling people to realize their full
potential speaks to your understanding that each
personality is unique. Through that understanding,
individual potential is fulfilled, objectives
are achieved, and success abounds.*

Di, you are truly an artist.

Contents

Introduction

The Science and Art of Management

Based on the title of this introduction, you may be thinking, *Why another book on this subject? I know what management is and what it requires.* However, this isn't your typical business tome, and the reference to science doesn't mean reviewing basics such as seeing increased productivity as the key to success. Nor does it indicate that I'll be rehashing technical tricks such as task-management orientation, focusing on objectives, or enforcing company rules.

The science that this book refers to is the study of human behavior and understanding the inherent traits of personality (our neurological hardwiring) that affect how we think; act; communicate; and perceive situations, experiences, and tasks. I'll focus on the fundamentals through understanding human nature and how it explains why people do what they do.

The second aspect of this subject is the art of management, which has to do with applying what you know about personality and using it in a way that harnesses people's inherent talents and strengths and creates an environment where everyone wants to succeed in a self-directed fashion, striving to reach optimal performance for *their* reasons, not yours.

This would certainly make everyone's job much easier, wouldn't it? Just think about folks working together in a cooperative manner toward a common objective; having the right individuals in the right jobs; minimizing the power struggles that surface because of personality differences; everyone being sensitive to each other's needs; having the freedom to share ideas, suggestions, and solutions; expressing appreciation; and feeling as if what they're contributing is making a difference.

Is this just a theoretical concept, or could it be reality? Actually, the answer to that question really depends on you and your focus as a manager and how you choose to use the information contained in the following chapters.

The Science of Personality

The research this book is based on is the *science of personality* and how it impacts who we are, how we think, how we act, and why we do the things we do. After studying the subject for more than 25 years, I utilized my own work as well as the teachings of Plato, Hippocrates, and Carl Jung to develop an understanding of the inherent part of human nature that's both predictable and observable—personality.

I refer frequently to *personality neurology* and the mental functioning associated with it to help create an awareness of how it influences decision making; affects the ways we learn; contributes to the formation of stress and tension; determines our perception of time and impacts how we manage it; and triggers misunderstandings and conflicts that build communication barriers, thus making it difficult for us to get on the same wavelength with the people in our lives.

These predispositions are the underlying causes of many of the struggles we experience in our interactions and show that contrary to what we might think or feel, people really aren't trying to make our life miserable. The friction arises because they truly don't see situations the same way we do. Consequently, if either person tries to impose their perceptions on the other, there's going to be a power struggle with someone trying to gain control. The bottom line is that one person wins and the other loses. This certainly doesn't foster a cooperative environment, nor does it create mutually satisfying relationships where everyone's needs are met.

The information contained in this book is a compilation of two different approaches—scientific and humanistic—both of which are intended to help expand your awareness of personality and its effects on every aspect of human behavior. The hard science includes the research and perspectives of personality neurology, neurobiology, neuropsychology, and the neurosciences, specifically focused on human consciousness. This also takes into consideration the latest research on the differences between the female and the male brain. Then there are what most consider to be the soft sciences, which include psychology, psychotherapy, and sociology.

The humanistic approach—and probably the easiest for us to relate to—consists of the insights offered by the many people who shared their stories; openly discussed their successes, struggles, and failures as managers; offered their perspectives; opened their hearts; and showed their true colors to add depth to this book so that what's offered within it is realistic, pragmatic, immediately applicable, and can truly make a difference in the way business is done. From my perspective, they've helped create a living classroom and taken what could have been a difficult and complex topic and turned it into an exciting and gratifying journey.

The Role of Personality

There's a tremendous amount of time, energy, and resources that are lost or misdirected when we don't understand the important role that personality plays in how we interact and engage with the people in our lives, both at work and at home. After all, it's our personalities that form the expectations we bring into our relationships and that influence why we choose to be around some people and not others. The better we can understand this natural part of who we are, the more we'll find that no one is as malleable as we'd like them to be.

It's true that some behavior is the result of conditioning and reflects others' perceptions and opinions of who we are and what we're capable of achieving, and that this is what forms many of the comfort zones and habits we create that add predictability to our lives. However, this isn't what I'll be addressing. Instead, I'll look at traits, the innate part of personality that forms the neurological hardwiring that tells the brain how to function, meaning how to gather and process information and make decisions. This is what can't be changed, what truly creates the behavior that's predictable and observable, and what remains so throughout our entire life. It surfaces the day we're born, and we display it consistently throughout our lives. This impacts and influences every aspect of our being.

Let me explain: If you rely on your five physical senses of sight, hearing, touch, taste, or smell to gather information, and what you discover must make sense before you can make a decision, then you'll use this process throughout your entire life. On the other hand, if you rely on your intuition and need to feel the *vibes* in order to figure things out, and you make decisions because they feel right, then you'll follow that pattern consistently over the years. In other words, the personality traits you're born with, you get to live with forever.

Now, to keep you from feeling boxed in, keep in mind that we can all learn to change the perceptions we have of ourselves and can acquire new interpersonal skills. We can even expand our consciousness, which will help us become whole-brain thinkers, but we can't alter the core essence of our personality neurology. Besides, it doesn't make sense to try, because that's what creates our natural talents and forms our inherent strengths.

The more we learn about the distinctions, the easier it will be for us to deal with people who are different from us and do so in a way that meets everyone's expectations. The ultimate benefit from understanding personality is that it reduces the amount of stress in our lives, which equates to better health and a more satisfying quality of life.

There are some underlying suppositions contained in this book that determined its structure and the materials presented:

- Personality traits define who we are and how we think, act, and communicate. They serve as the organizing principle behind behavior.

- Traits are instrumental in influencing how we interact with people and why we're attracted to some individuals and not others, and they create the expectations we bring into our relationships.

- Since there are different personality types, there are different perceptions of the same situation. It's these variations that become the source of misun-

derstandings and conflict, which cause the lines
of communication to break down.

- Traits influence how we adapt, our personal
growth, and our mental development.

- As there are various personality types, there are
different basic needs, strengths, values, and
motivations.

The premise of this book is to establish what I refer to
as *The Personality Approach to Management*, for it's through
the understanding of these ideas that a mediocre or inex-
perienced manager can become a great one, and how an
organization can create unified, talented, and self-reliant
teams of people who are supportive, loyal, dedicated, and
willing to rise to the occasion to achieve the desired results.
It creates an environment where people want to succeed
in their jobs rather than just showing up every day to get
their paychecks, where they can feel good about themselves because they're appreciated and respected, and where
there's the opportunity for them to reach their personal and
professional goals.

How Will You Identify Your Personality Type?

There's an assessment included in the book that will
enable you to identify your personality color, and in the
process may help you recognize those of the people in your
life, such as supervisors, peers, subordinates, associates, family members, and friends. You'll find a general description of
each of the four colors, as well as an in-depth look at their

management, leadership, communication, and teamwork styles. Also included is a list of the ten most predictable and observable behavioral patterns for each of the colors and an overview of the qualities that make them unique. Overall there's enough information to offer you a comprehensive look into each color and do so in a way that allows you to apply what you learn to the management process immediately.

Heightened Sensitivity

Any evaluation process that uses names, letters, behavioral pattern descriptions, or even colors (as I do) to explain personality types and their differences runs the risk of making people feel boxed in. I've tried to be sensitive to that fact and kept that concern foremost in my mind as I presented this information. I ask that you do the same and use this data with integrity and sensitivity. Here are some things to keep in mind:

- First and foremost, don't use the understanding of personality to discriminate. Prejudices of any kind are destructive to others and to yourself.

- Use the information to enhance the quality of your interactions and to increase your tolerance for differences.

- Rather than focusing on the negatives or deviations, look for similarities, and find ways to utilize the strengths that each person offers.

- When conflicts do arise, don't immediately assume that the other person is out to get you or to make your life difficult. They just see the situation differently.

- Use this information to find common discussion points. This will help focus on the issues and avoid personal attacks.

- Avoid using personality color as a means of defending behavior that's hurtful or harmful; don't use it to take advantage of someone.

In addition to personality traits, there are other factors that make us unique that shouldn't be overlooked. There are the differences between males and females, and those created by ethnic and cultural influences. As you move forward in this book, be mindful of what each person offers and the fact that it's not my intention to take away from that.

Regarding gender differences, because this book focuses on personality neurology, what's included applies to both males and females. And, while it's easy to assume that all people who make decisions based on emotional judgments—meaning how they feel—will be females, this isn't the case. Nor should it be assumed that everyone who acts on logic will be male, as this isn't true either. I've tried to isolate those differences as they pertain to the general understanding of personality typology and to eliminate the stereotypical behavior associated with the male/female roles. Please keep in mind that the intention of this book is to focus on the predictable and observable patterns associated with the inherent traits of personality and not on gender differences or the diversity of different cultures.

Finally, remember that there are no absolutes. We're all a reflection of societal conditioning, so the descriptions are intended to provide a general overview of each of the four types. The traits aren't meant to be restrictive or limiting, but instead are intended to be liberating and empowering. They're meant to be a point of reference and offer a non-threatening way to discuss differences and provide insight into yourself and those you interact with.

How to Use This Book

As you read, you'll see that every personality color contributes in its own unique way to the overall productivity in the workplace. You'll realize how different types can accomplish everyday tasks in varying ways, how some people are better suited for some tasks than others, and how they interact with others differently. You'll discover that while everyone has a preferred personality color based on their inherent neurology, few are completely one hue or another, and rather function as a rainbow based on the demands and expectations of their external environment. You'll be able to see the motives behind behavior and will learn how to incorporate them into your incentive plans and mentoring. And most important, you'll learn how to create teams of people who complement each other, enjoy working together, and produce exceptional results.

This book is divided into three main parts. Part I introduces the concept of the general approach to working with others and explains how personality influences the way we manage, interact with people, and do the things we do. Part II includes an assessment that will identify your color, as well as detailed descriptions of each of the four personalities. Part III is rich with practical information that you can put to immediate use. It looks at the most common management problems—communication and conflict, time and task management, and team building—and shares how each personality color sees the others. It also contains suggestions on how to use the information, do's and don'ts, and helpful hints, and clearly spells out how to interact with each of the four colors in specific situations. This will help you be a better manager, while at the same time reducing the amount of frustration and stress that comes along with the job of dealing with different kinds of people.

There's also an Afterword, which explores the attributes of successful people who apply the understanding of personality to their daily lives, and who discover in the process what they're capable of achieving. How innovative and exciting is that?

A Final Friendly Look at Personality

It's not my intention to offend anyone in this book. However, the ideas I share may do so, especially those whose emotional nature is to take things personally. I decided that rather than writing specifically to win friends, I'd rather impact people's lives and hopefully enhance their interactions and management experiences. The information is offered in a way that sheds light on both the positive and negative qualities of each of the four personality colors and portrays the real issues we all must deal with in our contact with those who aren't like us.

I wanted to write something that wasn't just a good read, but which would make a difference in people's lives. I hope what you'll learn will help you become more tolerant of, and more patient with, each other's idiosyncrasies and quirks, and maybe even more compassionate toward yourself. And most of all, I hope it will give you the tools that can help you excel in the art of management. The rewards are many.

Living Lives of Significance

As a Yellow personality, I've set high standards for this book and what it provides for you as the reader. The fundamental premise is that you find it informative and its information useful—more than just fluff and hype that looks good on paper but isn't applicable to your life. We live in a fast-paced world where people are being replaced by computerized functions and where business is conducted globally rather than in our own backyards. We can forget how important each individual is and how much we all need the element of human interaction, no matter what color our personality. And it's easy to become too busy or overloaded to remember the importance of expressing appreciation or to make the effort to put ourselves in others' shoes so that we can understand where they're coming from and be sensitive to how they're feeling.

I believe that to some extent we're all experiencing loss as we perceive less sensitivity and caring on the job, or for that matter, in the world. I believe we're searching to find the passion in what we do and trying to re-create a workplace that has spirit and where the needs of the people are as important as the bottom line. I believe that the key to finding what we're seeking lies in understanding people through the eyes of personality. For it's in this way that we'll make a difference and find ourselves living a life of significance.

Good luck and good managing,
Carol

PART I

THE PERSONALITY APPROACH TO MANAGEMENT

"The meeting of two personalities is like the contact of two chemical substances; if there is any reaction, both are transformed."

— Carl Jung

CHAPTER ONE

It's All about Effective Management

This is the fairy tale: In a hierarchical organization with a conventional chain of command, those at the top set the vision and issue the directives. Those in the middle interpret those directives and ensure that they're understood and followed, while those at the bottom do the work. Everyone understands their responsibilities as well as the corporate objectives and strives to perform their assigned tasks competently. The company runs smoothly and productively, achieving its goals . . . and they all live happily ever after.

And then we have the all-too-common reality: Those at the top, motivated by the desire for personal fame or fortune and driven by boards of directors, governmental regulations, stockholders, family needs, insecurity, greed, ego, indifference, or lack of knowledge, have their own vision of success. This goal is translated into directives ranging from micromanagement controls to vague references, which must then be transformed by intermediate managers into results-producing actions by those actually doing the work. Each person, from the top down to the bottom, sees, hears, responds, and otherwise communicates based on his or her unique personality.

Therein lies the ultimate challenge of management: communicating what needs to be done so that there's comprehension, and assessing results to stay on course to meet the desired objectives. Without effective oversight, success happens more through good luck than planning. Understanding personality is a key tool in achieving managerial effectiveness.

On the Job

The classical image of a manager is one who directs or supervises the activities of one or more people to accomplish the tasks necessary to achieve the objectives of an entity, business, or organization. On the job, the tasks of management have been delineated, described, debated, and damned in thousands of books, papers, lectures, training programs, and coaching sessions. Author Peter Drucker (1909–2005) was recognized by a significant number of the business leaders of his time as one of the greatest thinkers on this subject. He believed that success in a business environment was based on finding and training the best people available, because talented individuals were the key ingredient in every successful enterprise.

One of this country's leading corporations, during its major growth and expansion stages in the 1950s and '60s, operated under the Drucker concepts of recruiting from the top sources, hiring the best people in the labor market, providing them with exceptional training, rewarding them well for their achievements, and recognizing their achievements. The success and growth of that company reflected the effectiveness of this strategy. *The most essential assets of any successful business or organization aren't its products, facilities, equipment, or intellectual properties. They're its talented, well-trained, well-managed, appreciated, and productive people.*

The world of business, in all its diversity, operates in an inconsistent although predictable manner. There are the feudal dictatorships that function on the idea that employees are no more than serfs who will tolerate insensitivities and abuses because they can't find gainful employment elsewhere. Management in this environment is by tell or yell, seeking no feedback, engendering no loyalty, and creating a subculture of discontent that may show up in high absenteeism, low productivity, theft, vandalism, and even sabotage—all reflections of a payback-in-kind mentality on both ends of the structure.

Then there are the hierarchical businesses run in a quasi-military fashion. Here, the organization chart determines who can talk to whom. Orders are passed down the chain of command with little personalization or explanation of the whys behind the whats and whens. This model operates as if it were being run by a commanding general through high-ranking field officers with specific staff responsibilities, line managers with operational responsibilities, and troops in the field. There may be a half-dozen or more levels of management and staff, which frequently results in an information vacuum through which nothing can pass from the visionary at the top to the functionary at the bottom. The filters in the middle tend to remain forever clogged with territorial obsessions or self-serving perceptions of authority. Little gets through other than what these people allow; and the result is a loss of productivity, duplication of effort, and turf wars costing the business significant sums of time, productivity, and money.

Moving down the size scale, we find the entrepreneurial entity originated by an individual with a dream, concept, or love of a product or service. This can produce an exhilaration unsurpassed in the business world because it generally represents the fulfillment of a life's dream. Operating under this motivation, management tends to take on a paternal or maternal perspective with both the company and the employees. The expectation is that since the founder is in love with the venture, everyone working there will share that dedication and commitment.

That's often not the case, and the perceived need to micromanage may surface. Since the business becomes a part of the self-image of its creator, it must reflect his or her ethics or integrity and produce a product or service that measures up to that person's standards. It's easy for form to become the driving measurement here, rather than substance, and that impetus may erode the employee's perception of the owner's standards for the business.

Management staff in each of these situations faces challenges that differ, yet are also similar. Those in charge on the job, regardless of the size or scope of the entity, need to understand what must be done, when and how it's to be executed, and how its completion will be measured or evaluated. That most complex of tasks can be reduced to simple, consistent practices. Applying them is made more effective with an understanding of personality and its impact on the entire process.

In Everyday Life

The purpose of bringing the concept of management into our daily lives is that once we recognize it for what it is, our whole perspective changes. We're the managers of our fate, our ultimate destiny, how we choose to live, and what we're willing to tolerate in order to get what we want and need. There are no failures in life; there are only failures in managing our lives. For some personalities, that may sound cold and insensitive, while for others it will ring a loud, clear bell—therein lies a dichotomy of life.

If those willing to relegate supervision of their life journeys to others become disenchanted with their fate, who owns the responsibility? If those seeking to direct other people's life journeys become resented and disliked, who's to blame?

One of our true blessings as human beings is that we aren't all alike. We're one of two sexes; one of four personality colors; and one of myriad races, religions, and other beliefs. The mathematical permutations of those factors provide us with a world of unique and interesting people. Add to that the constantly changing environment, and we have a management challenge—not *of* a lifetime, but one that *fills* a lifetime.

A Final Reality Check

How you cope with self-management is strongly influenced by your personality traits. As you'll discover in subsequent chapters, your need to take charge of yourself—as well as your capacity to do so—is largely dictated by how you gather and process information and how you make decisions. Those qualities define your personality. For example, time sensitivity is of prime importance to one color and of little consequence to another. Therefore, each one prioritizes different tasks and doesn't understand the other color's choices. This can really be a problem when it comes to meeting deadlines!

Management in our personal world isn't consciously perceived as a responsibility. It's typically addressed as our basis for survival in a world that commands—yea, *demands* our responsiveness, or we pay a severe price in time, money, credibility, or acceptability. Think of the impact on our lives if we failed to effectively manage our personal cleanliness and grooming, temperament, or time commitments. Society quickly imposes a penalty for any of those shortcomings. Our options then become: Are we willing to pay that price, or is it too high?

We manage to survive . . . when we manage our lives. If we were to summarize the impact of supervising ourselves and the working world, we could say that it's the fuel that drives the productivity engine that produces the results that make our world viable. And if it's that important, then the more we can understand about it, the richer and more fulfilling our lives will be. We can all manage that.

❋ ❋ ❋

CHAPTER TWO

When All Else Fails, Refer Back to Personality

Ralph R. was recruited out of college as a sales rep for a large office-furniture manufacturer. He was a competitive athlete who played football for four years (although not well enough to go to the NFL). The hiring team was attracted by his drive to excel and his inherent motivation to succeed, regardless of the level of competition or the odds against him. He'd had to work his way through college with a nighttime job and lived in a dorm where costs and accommodations were modest at best. Ralph convinced the recruiters that once he accepted a set of sales objectives or quotas, he'd achieve or surpass them, no matter what obstacles surfaced along the way. The team liked his self-confidence, determination, and straightforward commitment to success.

Ralph delivered as promised. By his third year in the job, he was the leading salesperson in the company; by his fifth year, he was promoted to the position of senior sales rep, and two years later to territorial sales manager. He truly understood what it took to succeed, and he was confident that he could apply that understanding in his latest role, making his territory the top one in the company. He made a commitment to the corporate sales manager to do so.

The first three months were pure fun. He made customer calls with each of his salespeople, and using his product and closing experience, helped them bring in more business in their territories than ever before. Ralph was flying high and again standing out because of the fruits of his labors.

Then three of his top sellers asked to be transferred. They met with Ralph's boss and complained that Ralph had taken all of the joy out of their jobs because he persisted in making all of the important sales calls with them and elbowed them out of the way in front of their customers. They were humiliated by his domineering style. While they appreciated the increased commissions that they were being paid, the money wasn't worth the cost of losing face with their clients or giving up their feelings of personal accomplishment. Ralph wasn't managing; he was *doing* their work, serving as the ultimate order closer.

While the results were appreciated, the method wasn't. So Ralph was told to stay out of the field and to allow his staff to do the work they were hired for. Smarting from what he perceived to be an unfathomable demand, he initiated a series of reporting controls requiring daily documentation of each sales call, its results, and forecasts of orders to be closed. He moved from interfering directly to being a micromanager because it was the only way that he knew to control everything and everyone under his management responsibility.

Ultimately, Ralph left that position and returned to selling, the one job he really felt comfortable with. He never did figure out that management meant understanding the individual potential of each of the members of his sales staff and providing them the opportunities to develop that potential in the performance of their jobs.

Taking Care of Business

Olivia O. was a superb organizer. She finished college with a 3.8 grade point average and a community-service record that filled two pages. She served on every school committee that concerned itself with the well-being of humankind, for her primary focus in life was to make this a better world in which to live. She intended to follow that commitment when she graduated, so she accepted a position as the administrative assistant to the CEO of a very "green" company that produced environmentally safe cleaning products. She loved her job and the dedication of the organization to the ideals that she so strongly believed in.

After several years in that position, Olivia's ability to manage complex activities and events with style and class became evident. Little was done by the CEO that Olivia didn't set up, run, and control flawlessly; she was truly phenomenal. Thus, it was no surprise to anyone when she was promoted to the position of manager of finance and administration with the responsibility for all the support functions in the headquarters location. It was a job that she was totally qualified for.

As a manager, Olivia's first concern was her staff. Were they happy in their work? Was their health and that of their families good? Did they have the resources to do their jobs successfully? She was truly a people person. If there was anything that they didn't want to do or that caused them stress, she took it on herself and did it for them. Gradually, her employees began to recognize that they could delegate any unpleasant tasks up to her by whining and complaining, and she'd relieve them of that responsibility and take it on personally.

Within a year, Olivia found herself putting in 12-hour days and frequently six- or seven-day weeks trying to stay up with the workload. It took a toll on her family life and started to affect her health. She grew concerned but didn't want to complain to her boss because she loved the job and its responsibilities. However, it was making her sick—and worse yet, it was forcing her to choose between taking care of her personal family and taking care of her work family. She felt torn in half and guilty for not devoting more time to being the caretaker for each of the two groups she felt responsible for.

Ultimately, Olivia collapsed under the load and was put on a medical leave of absence. When she was back on her feet, she opted to become a stay-at-home mom and not return to the business world until her children were grown and on their own. Caring for two demanding families in the manner that she felt appropriate was just too much.

The Problem Solver

Yoshi Y. grew up in a large city with mixed cultural roots. While in high school, he tended to spend more time studying than socializing with his peers, and was considered standoffish, bordering on geeky. His diligence paid off when he graduated at the head of his class and earned a full scholarship to a major university. He majored in engineering and proved to have an exceptional aptitude for electronics, leading him to the world of computer science. While still in college, he designed a new process to enhance the production of chips used in laser applications. This earned him significant attention in that field and, upon graduation, a high-paying job with a company that developed laser products for the communications industry.

Yoshi loved working in the lab and having access to both his innovative peers and the tools to stimulate his mind.

As his experience grew, so did his achievements. Given a set of specs from a customer, he was able to create new and unique solutions to fill them. His social skills remained relatively unimportant, so he worked by himself most of the time. His preference was to be assigned a challenge and then to be left alone while he worked out the perfect solution in his head and subsequently took it from the computer to the finished product.

The CEO of the company, himself an engineer, wanted to recognize these contributions and achievements, so he approached Yoshi about stepping up to a position as manager of the design lab. Yoshi declined, explaining that his interests and abilities lay in working in his own head, not through others.

What Yoshi did offer, however, was that he'd jump at the opportunity to become the manager of an unsolvable-problems department, if that should ever be created. In that capacity, given time to think, he could assist any of his peers when they hit a wall on a project they'd been assigned. He'd have no direct managerial responsibility or accountability but would be able to contribute substantively to the success of the company and feed his own perspective of personal success. It was more important to him to solve a challenge than to wield power or control on the job. To make a historical comparison, he'd rather have been viewed as a Thomas Edison than a Thomas Jefferson.

Yoshi honestly—and realistically—perceived himself as a manager of things rather than people. He had a clarity of vision and self-understanding. He refused to put himself in a position of personal compromise for money or status.

Creating Opportunity

Gordon G. was a born artist. When he was a child, his ability to capture images and emotions on paper set him apart from others in his age group. He thrived on praise and recognition and continued to develop his talents through high school. By the time he was in college, his interests had expanded to sharing this gift with others and helping them discover and develop their own artistic gifts. While he truly enjoyed creating works of art, what he loved even more was the discovery of a creative gift in others and helping them reach the fullness of their potential.

As he moved into the working world in a graphic-design studio, he was able to fulfill both his creative and financial needs. Life was good, and that served him well as he expanded his knowledge of the business and eventually led him to becoming a partner in the firm where his career began.

Gordon's responsibilities included finding and working with talented freelance designers and overseeing their creative output for the studio. No one who knew him could imagine that there was a man more suited for, or happier with, the job than he was. Many of the people he helped develop won awards in industry competitions, and Gordon shared their triumphs like a proud father.

The key to his success was situating himself in a position where he worked at tasks he loved and excelled at, and that gave him the ability to express himself freely with few constraints on his productivity. As a manager, he was able to develop, inspire, and stimulate latent abilities in those who freelanced for him. He fully utilized his personality traits in a position where there were minimal guidelines and only deadlines to contend with. And while he didn't like being tied to a schedule, Gordon recognized that weakness and surrounded himself with time-oriented people who kept him on target. Life continued to be good.

Yes, Management Works

The perception that management can and does work exists in the minds of most managers—past, present, and future. It's a concept born at the dawn of humankind when the burden of tasks exceeded the capacity of one person to accomplish them. It was perpetuated through the ages as civilization demanded productivity beyond the capabilities of the individual.

Without some form of oversight, chaos reigns, which limits the growth and evolution of civilization. Management has been the key to our evolutionary progress from the primitive to the contemporary and the foundation for the development of our society. Why then does its value continue to be questioned? Is it because we fail to recognize that personality differences prevent us from understanding that there are multiple definitions of management emanating from each of the colors? Until we can recognize and accept those variations, supervisory practices will continue to be challenged. What we may have in their place could be autocratic domination, bullying, insensitivity, overcontrol, intimidation, or self-serving practices masquerading as management. Not a pretty picture however you view it.

The question then is: *What truly is effective management, and what tools are available to help us harness its potential for everyone's benefit?*

People Do Things for Their Own Reasons

In trying to understand human behavior, there's a basic principle that applies to all our actions: *People do things for their reasons and not ours.* Another way to say it is: *Other people see things, respond, and react in different ways. They'll usually do what they think will offer them the greatest reward for their efforts.*

What this means is that no one in a position of power can motivate others to work unless they understand which motivation factors produce the results they seek. Okay, sure, people will make a halfhearted effort if they're threatened, but all this does is produce marginal results; and it also ends up creating frustration, resentment, rebellious behavior, and power struggles.

If, as a manager, you can keep in mind that motivation is individualized and comes from within, it will make your job a lot easier. How? Because then all you have to do is create an environment where people, of their own accord, will want to cooperate, produce the desired results, and optimize their own performance.

By merely integrating this understanding alone into your management style, you'll significantly reduce the amount of friction, tension, dissent, stress, and upset; as well as the potential for misunderstandings, miscommunication, and conflict. You'll also find that people will naturally develop a sense of pride in the work they perform. On the other hand, if you don't incorporate this basic concept, there's a very good chance that you'll continue to be caught off guard when dealing with others, and may repeatedly find yourself embroiled in some sort of power struggle.

A good manager knows that people need to feel accepted for who they are, long to be recognized for their contributions, and want to enjoy themselves when interacting with their peers or superiors. A wise supervisor remembers the importance of the individual and knows that when folks feel good about themselves, they'll naturally reach higher standards in their performance and be motivated for their reasons and not yours. An intelligent person uses this information to help others become more productive and effective in what they do.

Traits Versus Characteristics

Personality has two aspects:

1. Inherited behavior *(traits)*
2. Learned behavior *(characteristics)*

When combined, they form what's referred to as *personality type.* However, there's a significant difference between the two aspects: Traits *can't* be changed because they're the fixed part of one's neurological hardwiring, and characteristics *can* be changed since they're acquired through external influences and experiences.

Traits

Traits are responsible for telling our brain how to develop and function, meaning directing it in gathering and processing information and making decisions. Traits are what drive the choices we make and how we decide to put them into action. Our behavior then tells other people how to interact and communicate with us, and defines how we'll deal with them. Traits determine how we learn and utilize our intuition. They regulate our problem-solving preferences and define our perception of what constitutes trouble. Consequently, they also influence the kinds of solutions we're most apt to create. In addition, traits are responsible for:

- Establishing our value system, the principles and core beliefs that serve as our code of conduct, and producing the behavior we use to support them

- Developing our natural talents and influencing how they're expressed

- Generating our perceptions, both internally and externally, and influencing what we do with them

- Directing our emotional reactions and our rational responses to experiences and situations

- Determining what motivates and irritates us

- Choosing the people we're attracted to and those we'll have a natural tendency to avoid

Characteristics

Characteristics refer to our learned behavior, the stuff that reflects our conditioning—meaning other people's perceptions, opinions, criticisms, social expectations, and experiences. They're responsible for the formation of the learned habits, attitudes, and comfort zones that ultimately impact our quality of life.

The motivation behind the development of characteristics is primarily to make us behaviorally acceptable so
that we can fit into a social structure. However, in doing so
they're responsible for creating many of the false perceptions
we have of ourselves, the ones that inhibit what we become
and what we're capable of achieving.

For example, if you were repeatedly told as a child that
you'd never be good at something, you'd begin to believe
it, thus creating limitations and insecurities around your
capabilities. The result would be that throughout your life,
you'd probably avoid engaging in any activities that might
bring those insecurities to the surface.

There's an interesting aspect to the behavioral patterns
created by characteristics. They're the mental barriers and
insecurities that in many cases are stronger than our ability
to overcome them. Consequently, we may not bring our
natural talents and strengths into expression. In addition,
characteristics are responsible for:

- Overriding our innate decision-making preferences, thus causing us to make choices for other
  people's reasons rather than our own

- Driving us to stay in situations, relationships,
  jobs, and lifestyles that are limiting and unhealthy
  because that's what's expected of us

- Suppressing our individuality and uniqueness

- Encouraging us to follow the path of least
  resistance

- Creating fears and insecurities

- Behaving in certain ways based on environmental requirements such as gender roles

- Spending time developing responsibilities and tasks that may not be well matched with our personality traits

As you seek to understand more about personality, it's helpful to keep these three important factors in mind:

1. People want to fit in, and as a result will take on what they perceive to be the behavior norm for their environment—even if it isn't in alignment with their personality boundaries.

2. It's human nature to judge people based on first impressions that may not reflect the true nature of their personalities.

3. There's a natural tendency to compare other people's behavior with our own to determine whether their personality is compatible with ours.

However, if you understand that personality is more than what you see on the surface, then you'll have the opportunity to really get to know new acquaintances and discover their natural talents. You may realize that someone you misread initially is exactly who you've been seeking for a job, or is most compatible in a social relationship. You might even find yourself more appreciative of the differences in people because you'll recognize that their strengths are your weaknesses, and how those variations offer the greatest opportunity to create a dynamic team of self-motivated people.

The People Factor

The much-used saying "People are a company's most valuable asset" is as relevant today as it was the moment it was created. The reason is that even with all the changes in the way we work, the nature of business hasn't changed. It's still centered on relationships, meaning that people want to work with those who are attentive and sensitive to their needs, are willing to solve their problems, and take the time to create personal connections.

It's the staff who keeps clients coming back and helps retain their loyalty even in transitional or difficult times; and it's these relationships that encourage customers to tell their family, friends, and co-workers to consider working with a company. The fact is that people are the determining factor in the success of any organization and make the difference between a mediocre company and an outstanding one. So it's just plain good business to want to invest in their personal development and create ways to harness their strengths and talents.

While productivity and managing information has become the norm in today's corporate environment, it's really the interactions among customers, vendors, and employees that give a company its competitive edge and differentiate it in this ever-changing global economy. This requires an organization and its management team to know their people at all levels in the hierarchical chain, and to create an environment where everyone feels like colleagues rather than subordinates. In doing so, they foster a team that's self-motivated and cooperative and looks forward to coming to work.

Every day, there are articles in newspapers and business magazines about companies that have failed because they forgot the importance of people and placed more emphasis on their own individual needs. In reading about the fallout of their actions, it's difficult to understand how folks who have worked long and hard and invested their time, energy, and money can be forced to walk away with nothing.

It's even tougher to comprehend the results of a survey reporting that more than half of America's workforce believes that business is based on greed, lying, stealing, and doing whatever it takes to make a buck. No wonder stress-related workers'-compensation claims are skyrocketing, costing American businesses more than $160 billion annually in the falloff of productivity and increased absenteeism.

Going to work can be hazardous to your health, especially if you're with a company that places more value on the bottom line than it does on its staff. If we're to change the perception of business, then those in positions of power must become attuned to people's needs, take time to cultivate their individuality, and figure out what motivates them. Understanding personality is the first step, because it's where you'll truly gain insight into what makes everyone tick.

An Added Bonus

In addition to learning about other people and what they require, you'll gain a deeper understanding of yourself and discover more about what *you* need in order to achieve the success you desire. As you come to know yourself better and understand how your personality affects all aspects of your life, you'll begin to see yourself from a different per-spective—not from your conditioning, but rather from your inherent traits.

You'll finally make sense of why you're not good at some tasks and have a tendency to procrastinate rather than doing them. You'll understand why there are certain people you don't want to be around and why they grate on your nerves. This knowledge will put you in a better position to evaluate your relationships, career, and lifestyle so that you can change what isn't working—and do so confidently rather than out of desperation. It will be easier for you to let go of self-defeating patterns of behavior, fears, and insecurities because you'll realize that they're merely the result of your experiences and conditioning—not things you were born with.

Who knows, you might start appreciating yourself—all of you, not just some parts. You may find that the very things that other people criticize you for are your greatest assets. Perhaps what motivates you isn't the norm, and marching to your own drummer is positive rather than negative. You might even dare to finally follow your dreams rather than waiting until everything is just right—the right time, amount of money, or age.

If you can tuck this away in your head or your heart, it can save you great frustration, disappointment, and grief along the path of life. There are many ways in which you can learn more about who you really are. The healthiest and most successful method is to understand your personality. The most destructive and limiting option is to put yourself in a position where other people are in control of telling you who you are.

Not a difficult choice, is it?

※　※　※

PART II

THE FOUR
PERSONALITY COLORS

"I yam what I yam."
— Popeye

CHAPTER THREE

What Color Is
Your Personality?

Okay, now on to the really exciting stuff, like discovering what your personality color is and learning about your individual style: why you do the things you do, how you learn, your neurological hardwiring, your problem-solving habits, the way you communicate, and your management and leadership instincts. This is where you'll get to the root of your basic needs, strengths, irritations, values, and what causes you stress. And while you're learning about yourself, you'll be finding out the same valuable information about the people you work with or manage, as well as everyone else in your life. Yet you'll do so not from the perspective of labeling or name-calling, but from that of color—personality color.

However, before you begin, I must warn you that how you see and interact with people is about to change forever. I also need to caution you about the side effects that come along with your newly acquired awareness. They might include weight loss, as you'll spend more time people watching than eating; and there will also be staring, gawking, guessing, scoffing, disbelieving, acting like a know-it-all, and the uncontrollable urge to share what you know with others—even total strangers.

Additional consequences may be acceptance, amazement, compassion, empathy, increased sensitivity, appreciation, admiration, approval, and the uncontrollable desire to say thank you—thank you for being who you are, for a job well-done, for your contributions, for what you taught me, and for your perspectives. Meetings will never be the same, nor will any other interactions—team efforts, business lunches, cocktail parties, golf outings, bowling night, or ski trips. Everything is about to shift as your view of human behavior is transformed.

A Brief History of Personality Typology

Throughout history, there has been a tendency to categorize personality, for it offers a way to organize and simplify the complexities of human behavior. One of the first to use personality typology was Plato, who developed a system through which his students could understand the nature of human behavior. Others such as Hippocrates (considered the father of Western medicine) and Paracelsus used their beliefs about personality to help explain the nature of mental dysfunction and illness. Ever since these great thinkers declared their findings, many others have been intrigued, puzzled, and motivated to create a system that can help us understand why we do the things we do.

In the early 20th century, it was Swiss-born psychiatrist Carl Jung who suggested that the behavior associated with personality wasn't random, but in fact was both predictable and observable, and therefore could effectively be categorized. He suggested that the differences in how people act that were obvious even to the untrained eye were the result of preferences created by a person's neurological brain hardwiring rather than the result of their conditioning, and that this affected every aspect of life. Such preferences, Jung believed, are at the very core of human behavior and are intended to act as the attractors of experiences, as well as forming aversions toward some people, tasks, and particular events.

It should be noted that this work was in sharp contrast with that of his colleagues, who were still associating personality typology with learned behavior and psychological dysfunctions, such as mental illness and other anomalies.

In 1921, Carl Jung published his findings in the text *Psychological Types*, which outlined his four classifications of personality typology brilliantly and provided a fundamental understanding of human behavior. And while the book isn't an easy read, it states that people approach life experiences and see situations differently, and therefore will draw varying conclusions. Jung's understanding of typology not only changed the way actions are viewed, it expanded the perceptions of how individuals handle themselves in a variety of situations. His work provided a more reasonable way to look at those who are different from us, who don't fit our personality preferences or style. He offered insight into how to effectively interact with others when they don't share the same values or principles that we do.

Color . . . a Common Language

Color plays a far more powerful role in our lives than most of us imagine. It acts as both a perceptual and physical stimulus and affects all aspects of who we are, both internally and externally. It's as much a part of our daily existence as breathing, eating, and sleeping. We use this common language to describe how we feel and what we see: We say that we're blue when we're depressed, seeing red when we're angry, or green with envy. We even refer to ourselves as being yellow when we lack the courage to step up to a situation that needs attention. When describing what we see, we talk about the blue skies, the yellow rays of the sun, green forests, and golden fields of wheat. Physically, color also impacts us, as it can increase or decrease heart rate, raise or lower blood pressure, change breathing patterns, stimulate or suppress the desire to eat, affect hormones, and even influence concentration.

It seems that no matter what our gender, age, conditioning, or personality traits, color is our descriptive language of choice. We all relate to it in similar ways—it's a comfortable means of personal expression.

Using Color to Identify Personality Type

The criterion for any reliable personality tool is to provide information that's accurate, immediately applicable, and most important, easy to remember. When I first started out in this field and evaluated the different tests available, I found that while the information that many offered was accurate and applicable, the results were either difficult to remember or the identification process was vague, restrictive, or even unpalatable because it made people feel boxed in.

At that time, I was following a well-respected system that used the combination of letters to identify 16 different personality types. I was working with many different-sized companies, all the way from small family-run operations to Fortune 500 corporations. My services included business planning, workshops focusing on team building and effective communication, and training line managers.

It was my standard business practice to follow up with

my clients 30 days after a session to see how the process of using personality was working out. The significant majority of my feedback indicated that the information was valuable, it was a good investment, productivity had increased, they were spending less time dealing with people problems, and they found it easier to deal with individual differences. However, when I asked them what their personality letters were or the letters of those on their team, hardly anyone could remember. After many of these discussions, I decided that I needed to find a better and easier way for people to identify and remember their type.

In my quest to come up with a solution, I ran across the work of Dr. Max Lüscher, who used color to explain the different personality types. Dr. Lüscher believed that color had both an emotional and physiological value, and that a person's reaction to specific shades revealed their inherent personalities. His research, while not widely accepted among his peers, provided conclusive evidence that certain hues created the same emotional and physiological reaction in people who shared similar traits.

While acknowledging that the measurement of emotions wasn't completely possible, Dr. Lüscher based the reliability and viability of his findings on the measurement of physiological reactions. It was his work that ultimately led to my development of the Personality Color Indicator (PCI) in 1986. You'll soon be using the PCI to identify yourself via the perspective of color.

The Personality Color Indicator

Combining Dr. Lüscher's work with my own research and then applying my knowledge of the psychology of color,

31

I began to recognize how effective color is in describing human behavior. Then I created an overlay process, merging the predictability of personality traits with the certainty of behavioral responses to specific colors—taking into account the chemical and neurological changes created by both color and personality—and found that color was indeed an effective way to describe our variations as individuals.

There were other benefits as well: Color provided a non-threatening way to discuss differences so that hurt feelings and conflict were minimized, or in many cases eliminated completely. The discomfort people felt upon being labeled went away, as did the vagueness created by the use of numbers and letters, and the problem of everyone feeling boxed in was no longer an issue. Most important, I found that months, and even years, after taking the PCI assessment, people could still remember their color and were still talking in those terms. The four colors the PCI uses are Red, Orange, Yellow, and Green. These were chosen to represent the four personality types and don't indicate a personal preference for the actual shade.

It should be noted that while this is an effective way to describe personality type, it doesn't mean you're trapped into functioning in just one category. Sometimes situations and circumstances require that you move outside of your preferences in order to fit into your environment or get tasks done. While the purpose of the PCI is to identify your primary personality color as it relates to your traits, it is also intended to offer insight into the behavior of all the other types, too, so that when life requires you to move outside your usual orbit, you can do so without experiencing stress or feeling compromised. However, remember that while all colors can function outside their color preference for a short period, doing so for a long time may have an adverse impact on them both psychologically and physically.

Discovering Your Personality Color

Each of us holds an untapped potential that's just waiting for the right opportunity to express itself. One way to turn that possibility into reality is to deepen your understanding of who you are and why you do the things you do. Identifying your personality color is the first step in the exciting self-discovery process. Through knowing your color, you'll start to see yourself differently, and you'll begin to figure out why some of the things you've tried in your life have worked but others haven't. You'll understand why some people are easy to get along with, while others are difficult. You might even find yourself being able to read people more effectively both at work and at home. No matter how you choose to use the knowledge, you'll find your life rich with color. It will be as though you are looking through the lens of a kaleidoscope—lots of lovely hues, interacting differently with each change and always becoming more beautiful than before.

The assessment you're about to take is self-reflective, meaning that you don't need a psychological professional to administer it, score it, or interpret its findings. The PCI is self-scoring and very user-friendly. It consists of 60 statements, each of which is designed to talk to specific parts of your brain with the intention of revealing your personality traits. Once you determine your highest score, it will be associated with one of the four different colors: Red, Orange, Yellow, and Green.

The best approach when making your statement selections is to use this criteria: *Do you think or feel that the statement best describes you overall?* Respond to each item based on your first instinctive response and how you initially feel about what you've read. Don't get bogged down questioning whether you act one way at work and another at home.

Be as honest with yourself as you can—this isn't about winning a popularity contest. There's also no point in trying to deceive yourself or be someone other than who you really are. And for all of you analytical and logical personality types, don't spend a lot of time trying to psych out the assessment or manipulate its outcome. All this will do is cause confusion and get your mind to the point where it can't make a decision. One final reminder: There aren't any right or wrong choices, nor can you pass or fail. And contrary to what you might believe, everyone *does* have a personality!

Instructions for Taking the PCI

1. Read each statement carefully, and if it describes you and you agree with it, circle the letter to the left. It helps if you respond from the earliest recollections of how you were as a child, not from the perspective of who you've become as you've grown older.

2. If you don't relate to a statement, skip it and move on; you don't have to mark every one. In fact, if the words don't resonate for you, you'll have a natural hesitancy to circle the letter. When this occurs, it will be your traits talking, so don't mark that one.

3. Some personalities will consciously try to beat the assessment, while another type will look for patterns in order to skew the results. After 20 years of fine-tuning the PCI, I'll just say up front that because these statements talk to your brain, it's difficult to manipulate the results. Some people have taken it ten times or more with the thought of intentionally trying to change the final outcome, only to find out

that their personality color remains the same. In fact, what they usually discover is that their numbers get stronger in their color each time they take it. It seems that the more we learn about who we are, the less willing we are to become someone else.

4. Once you finish the assessment, follow the self-scoring directions. They'll help you determine your personality color.

The Personality Color Indicator

A 1. I consider myself to be down-to-earth.

A 2. I prefer to stick to a set daily routine rather than put myself in unfamiliar situations.

B 3. I enjoy using my creativity to come up with innovative ways of doing things rather than doing them the way that everyone else does.

A 4. I stay focused and concentrate on what needs to be completed now rather than thinking about future tasks.

B 5. I become bored with things that are repetitious and find myself looking for different and better methods of doing them.

B 6. I enjoy the challenge of figuring out solutions to problems that are complex and that need to be explored from a variety of perspectives.

A   7.   I consider myself to be practical, not theoretical.

B   8.   I have a lot of thoughts in my head simultaneously, and I'm often accused of not listening or of being preoccupied.

A   9.   I'd rather work with facts and figures than theories and ideas.

B   10.   I pride myself on using my intellect and being a creative problem solver.

A   11   I'd rather deal with the known than explore possibilities.

B   12.   I prefer being original rather than traditional.

B   13.   I'm interested in how machines and products work so that I can come up with ways to improve them.

B   14.   I prefer learning new skills more than using old ones.

A   15.   I'm detail oriented.

A   16.   I find myself attracted to people who are similar to me: realistic, practical, and involved with current issues.

A   17.   I become impatient and frustrated with problems or tasks that are too complicated.

B 18. I prefer to read books that provoke thought and allow the mind to wander and explore a variety of scenarios.

A 19. I'd rather follow standard operating procedures than create new ways of doing things.

A 20. I want work tasks and time expectations clearly defined before I begin a project.

B 21. I'm usually on a different wavelength than most people.

B 22. I tend to answer questions with another query in order to gather more information.

A 23. I interpret things literally rather than conceptually.

A 24. I'm more interested in the production and distribution of products than their design and application.

B 25. I thrive on variety and dislike repetition.

B 26. I'm a risk taker and shun the conservative approach to life.

A 27. I look for tried-and-true ways to solve problems and rely on past experiences rather than wasting my time seeking new and unproven solutions.

B 28. I enjoy listening to new ideas and exploring their potential rather than dealing with the mundane.

B 29. I'd rather create with my mind than produce with my hands.

A 30. When confronted with a problem, I react quickly rather than dwelling on it before doing anything.

D 31. I'll suppress my own feelings rather than hurt others.

D 32. I go overboard for people and overextend myself to meet their needs, even at my own expense.

C 33. I don't show my feelings easily and have been told that I'm hard to get to know.

C 34. I'd rather deal with task challenges than people problems.

C 35. I resolve conflicts based on what's fair rather than being concerned with feelings.

D 36. I find that people tend to take advantage of my good nature and kindheartedness.

C 37. I react with logic rather than emotion.

C 38. I rarely seek advice from others before I make a decision.

C 39. I'm critical by nature and express my opinions freely.

D 40. I warm up to people easily and wouldn't want to be thought of as cold and indifferent.

D 41. I prefer a work environment where there's no conflict and where people are appreciated and praised for what they contribute.

C 42. I make decisions based on logic rather than emotions.

D 43. I show my feelings easily.

D 44. I'm accepting (rather than judgmental) of others.

D 45. I expect those close to me to be sensitive to my feelings and emotional ups and downs, and I feel hurt when they aren't.

D 46. I resolve conflicts by asking people for their advice so that I can gain reassurance and confidence in my decisions.

C 47. I stay calm, cool, and collected in situations where others are reacting emotionally.

D 48. I'm good at resolving people problems.

C 49. I'm a perfectionist and like things done the right way—my way.

C 50. I'm more task oriented than people oriented.

D 51. I'm more concerned with making good decisions than the right decisions.

C 52. I'd rather work with someone who's reasonable and responsible than with someone who's thoughtful and kind.

D 53. I'm a peacemaker, not an aggressor.

D 54. I tend to be overly sympathetic to the needs of others.

C 55. I'm more interested in solving problems than dwelling on them.

C 56. I deal with people issues in a straightforward manner and call them like they are.

D 57. I believe that it's important to promote good feelings and harmony within my relationships.

C 58. I think that it's more important to be respected than to be liked.

D 59. I'm good at creating a team atmosphere and getting others to rally around a common goal or cause.

C 60. I show how much I care for someone by being responsible and conscientious rather than emotional and sentimental.

Self-Scoring Key

Total the letters circled.

_____ Total A's   _____ Total B's
_____ Total C's   _____ Total D's

Add **A** and **C** together and place that total below under RED.

Add **B** and **C** together and place that total below under YELLOW.

Add **A** and **D** together and place that total below under ORANGE.

Add **B** and **D** together and place that total below under GREEN.

RED   **YELLOW**

A + C _____   B + C _____

ORANGE   **GREEN**

A + D _____   B + D _____

Interpreting the Scores

While each of us regularly uses all of the mental pro-cesses identified in the Personality Color Indicator, we're primarily driven neurologically by the mental functioning of only one of the four colors. This one, identified through the highest score, represents your core personality traits, which again determines how you gather and process information and make decisions. It's also this primary color that drives what motivates you, determines your inherent and instinctive behavior, and influences how you interact with other people.

The second highest number and the color associated with it represent what's called your *coping personality.* This is what you might find yourself using to fit into a world that marches to a different drummer than you do. It's a reflection of your characteristics, meaning the learned behavior created by the external influences of conditioning.

If your highest number is in Green or Orange, it indicates that you make decisions based on how you feel—you use your emotions to judge if something is right or wrong for you. If your number is highest in Red or Yellow, it indicates that you make decisions based on logic and reasoning and prefer the analytical approach.

Should you find that you have the same highest scores in two colors, I suggest that you read the descriptions for each of the personality colors, highlighting what you can relate to as you go along. It will quickly become obvious what your primary color is.

Just because two or more numbers are the same for you doesn't mean that you have multiple personalities. The PCI isn't an instrument for measuring psychological dysfunction. It just means that you're flexible and adaptable or are in an intense time of change and personal growth. It's also important to keep in mind that when your color doesn't match how you see yourself or who you want to be, it may indicate that you've actually grown so accustomed to operating from your characteristics rather than your traits that you've lost sight of who you really are.

If your score is particularly high in one color—meaning

that there's more than a five-point spread between your highest number and the next one down—it reflects that you function primarily from your traits. So when you're required to step outside of them, you'll have to consciously make the choice to do so.

If all of your numbers are close—meaning within one point of each other—it can mean that you're flexible and adaptable or that you're in a time of change and unsure of the direction you should go. It should also be noted that if your personality color is Green, it's not unusual for your numbers to be close because this color is the chameleon of the personality world. By nature, Greens are so inherently flexible and adaptable that they'll appear to change constantly. In other words, they're very adept at taking on the behavior of the people they're interacting with or whatever they feel is needed to help them complete their tasks. While this is a wonderful quality, it's important for them to go back to their true nature each day, which means creating activities that encourage them to just be themselves. As Kermit the Frog said, "It's not easy being green"—that is, unless you do wonderful things that help you discover how great it is.

Most important, if you find yourself feeling any discomfort or confusion as a result of the assessment, go back and read the descriptions of each of the four types. This will help you uncover your traits and find your true color.

The Neurology of Personality

Some people are born left-brain dominant, some are born right-brain dominant, and then there are others who use one side to gather information and the other side to make decisions. Yet interestingly, all of these folks can come to the same conclusion—it's just that they use different neurological pathways to get there.

The brain dominance we're born with is believed to be reflective of our inherent personality traits. From a neurological perspective, traits primarily determine how we naturally tend to gather information and process information, solve problems, and relate to our experiences. They form the mental defaults that the brain will automatically resort to when evaluating information and deciding what to do with the data.

In his work, Carl Jung determined that predictable and observable human behavior roughly corresponds to two or more of the four quadrants of the brain, and that each personality type would employ some combination of them for the purpose of gathering information and making decisions. He referred to this process as Distinct Modes of Psychological Functioning.

The statements of the PCI you just completed spoke to each of these sections in a way that asked them to reveal your preferred combination, which determined your personality color. When the statement matched your preference, you probably found it easy to respond, and when it didn't there was a natural tendency to skip ahead. Some sentences spoke specifically to the people who cross over in their mental functioning, so if this wasn't your preference, then the words would be confusing or appear redundant. Again, the tendency would be to move on to the next item.

By understanding the neurological preferences for each of the four personality colors, it will become obvious why people are different, and you'll clearly see how those variations impact the interactions between people. I ask you to put on your manager hat—and when appropriate, your personal-relationships hat—for what you're about to learn can apply to every aspect of your life.

Four Quadrants—Four Different Perceptions

Each quadrant of the brain offers a different perception of the same information. When your preferred combination is engaged, a comprehensive picture of how to use that information is provided. The outcome is that the data gathered is reliable and the decisions made are in alignment with your personality traits, thus producing the results you desire. Quadrants A and B are part of the gathering process, and Quadrants C and D are part of the decision making.

PROCESSING CENTERS

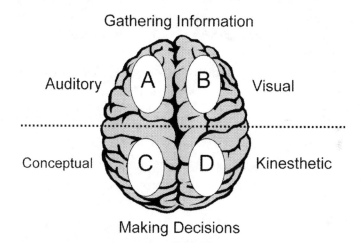

Gathering Information

Auditory   A   B   Visual

Conceptual   C   D   Kinesthetic

Making Decisions

Quadrant A (Left Frontal)

Personality colors who favor this quadrant rely on their five physical senses for the gathering of information, meaning that if they can't see, hear, touch, taste, or smell it, then the data isn't valid. Quadrant A processes information as black or white, tangible, and matter-of-fact. There are no abstract or gray areas in this part of the brain. This quadrant takes everything literally and will only use what it can relate to, meaning things that are familiar and can be backed by some historical precedent.

This quadrant deals well with details and facts and prefers to stick with what's tried-and-true. Consequently, its tendency is to dismiss or negate any information that it can't relate to and to resist new things or taking risks until it can gather the appropriate support. When it gets the needed evidence, it not only supports change—it charges ahead. This part of the brain recognizes the need to grow.

Personality colors that employ this quadrant as part of their mental functioning can get bogged down readily in everyday trivia and may have trouble taking action if this part of the brain becomes overwhelmed with too much incoming information that it can't relate to. Those who favor this quadrant are methodical, realistic, analytical, mathematical, and pragmatic.

Quadrant B (Right Frontal)

Personality colors who favor this quadrant are strongly visual and rely on their intuition, sixth sense, and "vibes" for the gathering of information. It's as if they somehow feel things rather than relying on the five physical senses to provide feedback. Quadrant B is freewheeling and views information holistically rather than breaking it down into bite-size pieces. It also processes input randomly, rather than sequentially as required by Quadrant A.

This part of the brain looks for the patterns and similarities and uses those factors to connect the dots, meaning determining if the information is viable and usable. It prefers abstract over black-and-white and deals effectively with gray areas, for it's there that this quadrant is able to generate new ideas and possibilities and come up with alternative solutions.

This processing of information tends to jump from one subject to another. It doesn't become burdened with details and is open and receptive to change. Quadrant B is responsible for recognizing what needs to change. Personality colors who favor it tend to be risk takers, have rich imaginations, become easily bored with redundancy, and prefer seeking new experiences and new ways of doing things rather than sticking with what's tried-and-true.

Quadrant C (Left Midbrain)

Personality colors who favor this quadrant for decision making are logical, analytical, disciplined, and rational, with the need for organization and structure. They're good at creating processes, procedures, and systems. Quadrant C is the thinking part of the brain and requires the time to consider things before it can proceed in the decision-making process. It requires evaluating and weighing all of the options, and if it gets bogged down with too many options or details, it can become mentally immobilized.

Quadrant C needs information to be presented in an orderly, linear, sequential, and impersonal manner so that it can ensure that the decision it makes will address the problem thoroughly. Data must make sense and the ramifications associated with the solutions it creates must be fully weighed—in other words, this part of the brain must thoroughly understand something before it can act upon it.

It's continually searching for the relationships and values in experiences and asks questions as a means of ensuring that the input it receives is reliable. This quadrant needs to understand the "what and how" before it can act. It's responsible for making the best choices to ensure that the changes being made are the right ones.

Personality colors who favor this part of the brain tend to be unwilling to waver in their decisions; are strongly opinionated, judgmental, and critical; and often play devil's advocate as a means of validating information. They function best with goals and objectives, a plan of action, and a timeline.

Quadrant D (Right Midbrain)

Personality colors who favor this quadrant for decision making are emotional and focus on people and the human connection. They're sensitive, caring, and compassionate and tend to follow their hearts rather than their heads.

Quadrant D uses emotional judgments to determine if the information it receives is good and can be relied upon or if it's bad and shouldn't be acted on. It personalizes everything as a means of evaluating how the decision it creates is going to affect other people. It wants to know the "why" before it can draw any conclusions and isn't interested in the "how or what." This thinking process is subjective and seeks to understand the interconnectedness between what it receives externally and how it feels internally.

Quadrant D is responsible for initiating the willingness to change. Personality colors who favor it have the need to express their feelings, are emotionally sensitive, have a strong desire to avoid conflict, and function best in environments where there's peace and harmony.

It Really Is All in the Mind

As you can see from the brain-quadrant explanations, what makes us different is really all in the mind. Consequently, it's only natural for us to see things differently, have varying opinions, and come up with multiple solutions. It's also easy to understand why it's so difficult to get on the same wavelength with another person if they don't gather information or make decisions in the same way.

If you can remember that everything people do is based on perception, and everyone *perceives* differently and as a result *processes* differently, then it will be easier for you to create a working environment that allows each person to mentally function within his or her preferred brain quadrants. The result is less stress, increased productivity, more effective communication, and fewer power struggles.

※　※　※

CHAPTER FOUR

The Red Personality: It's All about the Bottom Line

The information in this chapter is intended to offer a comprehensive overview of the Red personality that can be used as a reference guide. It's presented from a pragmatic perspective for dealing with superiors, interacting with peers, or supervising subordinates. It's intended to be both useful and directly applicable. I've addressed the most relevant aspects of the Red's behavioral patterns and neurology—including personality, learning, management, communication, and teamwork styles—and have concluded with a brief summary that can be easily accessed when a situation doesn't warrant a lengthy explanation.

Reds at a Glance

Reds are naturals to assume positions of authority, as their talents lie in leadership, administration, facilitation, and execution. The business world is their domain and offers them the greatest opportunity for success. They're natural managers, and they're most apt to reach their full potential at the helm of a business or in an organizational power position. You can always count on Reds to have the facts, to manage details with ease, and to be well informed regarding what has worked and what hasn't. They're diligent and responsible and work hard at whatever they do. These no-nonsense, conscientious, competent, intense people pride themselves on their high standards and work ethics. They wield power in a straightforward manner and seldom back away from a challenge or a project.

Reds are pragmatic and effective in conserving and managing resources, setting priorities, and delegating. Their contributions include bringing a sense of order, structure, and predictability to the office. In return, they want their job responsibilities to be well defined and to know how their performance will be measured. They want a workplace that's stable and consistent in its policies. They want to know that the organization will support them and their decisions, and they need a sense of job security.

Reds don't like surprises. If changes occur too fast, if they're blindsided or kept out of the loop, or if they don't agree with the new program, they'll become edgy, uncooperative, antagonistic, and even aggressive. The result is that this color will compensate by becoming overly controlling and going into a micromanaging mode. When any of these behaviors surface, they're warnings to other people to back off and give Reds the space they need in order to work out their frustrations.

Ten Predictable Behavioral Traits of a Red Personality

Here are ten of the most predictable and observable traits of the Red personality. Each of these contributes to their strong-minded nature and their take-charge persona. Although other personality colors may display what appear to be similar behaviors, a Red will demonstrate them more consistently and frequently.

1. Controlling. Being in control is the only way in which Reds can function, because otherwise there's chaos, which is mentally destructive to them. Their take-charge personality and their need to be in charge make them the perfect candidates to take on responsibilities associated with power and authority. As a means of gaining control of a situation, Reds will intimidate others by raising their voices, becoming verbally explosive, and using whatever tactics are necessary to ensure that people won't challenge them or question their authority.

2. Competitive. Reds aren't hesitant, squeamish, or fainthearted when it comes to doing whatever it takes to come in first; nor are they the type of personality to cheer for or side with the underdog. They want to associate with winners because that's how they see themselves. People in this color group enjoy creating competitive situations where there can only be one victor. Should you find yourself in competitive situations with Reds, remember that someone is going to lose—and they're convinced that it's not going to be them. This means that they'll continue to press on until they're sure that victory is theirs. They won't stop until they get what they want. Their attitude with respect to competition is "If you can't take the heat—stay out of the kitchen."

3. Methodical. Reds believe that the only way to move forward with anything is in a sequential, step-by-step, and logical manner. They understand the need for rules and procedures because that's the only way for them to maintain control and ensure that goals and objectives are met. Reds pride themselves on their production at work, and they see repetition and routine as part of the process of getting from point A to point B.

4. Explosive. The volatility of Reds is exhibited quickly and frequently. Their explosive nature can be intimidating and unsettling and may catch people off guard, thus causing them to become submissive and timid. Temperamental outbursts are the Reds' way of gaining control over a situation and preventing others from challenging their authority. Depending on the level of frustration or degree of anger, these emotional displays may range from yelling to throwing objects to hitting something or someone. The difficulty in dealing with Reds who are angry is the uncertainty of how violent the situation will become or how long it will last.

5. Orderly. Reds need to be organized and to live a structured life in order to be productive and feel good about themselves. They want everything in its place and expect other people to put things back where they belong after using them. They can be obsessive-compulsive in their need for tidiness and a set daily routine. Reds have a difficult time functioning in an environment that's cluttered, chaotic, or emotionally volatile. Their craving for order drives them to be the ultimate list makers and to rely on productivity aids such as daily planners, PDAs, and cell phones to help manage their lives, thus minimizing chaos and preventing things from falling through the cracks.

6. Demanding. Reds have dogged determination and are relentless in their drive to meet their objectives. They approach everything in a no-nonsense, straightforward, and matter-of-fact way. They take all tasks and projects seriously and instinctively look for the most efficient way to do things. Reds are hardheaded and hard-nosed and won't take no for an answer. They're demanding of both themselves and other people.

7. Conscientious. Whether it's satisfying the objectives of their jobs or fulfilling the needs of their families, Reds are willing to do whatever it takes. They're dedicated, reliable, diligent, and intensely focused. No matter what they take on, they always work hard at it and strive to do their best. They want to do things right and are willing to devote as much time as is needed to ensure a favorable outcome.

8. Realistic. Reds are down-to-earth and have their feet firmly planted on the ground. They're sensible and practical—no pie in the sky or head in the clouds for them. They see things for what they really are versus what other people would like them to be. The Reds' motto is "What you see is what you get." They don't have the time or inclination to create things that won't solve an immediate problem or aren't functional, or to jump on ideas or schemes that don't have a proven track record for producing the results they want.

9. Resistant to change. Reds will fight change tooth and nail if they can't see how it will benefit them. They'd rather stay with what's tried-and-true than take a chance on something new. They won't embrace a shift in action or policy just because someone else tells them that they must or that it's the right thing to do. Reds want to see the facts that support the need for a switch, and then they'll ask for a guarantee that the new system will work. If they don't get what they need to justify the modifications, they won't go along, but instead will dig their heels in.

10. Disciplined. Reds are the most self-disciplined of all of the personality colors and it shows up in every aspect of their lives—their daily routines, their general lifestyle, how they adhere to the rules, and their "stick with it" approach. However, where it shows up most is in getting the job done. They focus on results and set high performance standards that they expect others to follow. Whether they're working or playing, people in this color establish schedules and form habits that drive what they do and when and how they do it.

Personality Style

RED PERSONALITY

Auditory   A   Visual

Conceptual   C   Kinesthetic

The Reds' personality-quadrant-combination preference is A and C. This means that they're left-brain dominant, so information must make sense before they can move into the decision-making process; and once they do so, they're methodical, logical decision makers. They depend on quadrant A to break the information down into bite-size pieces, and then use quadrant C to reconstruct it in a step-by-step process. They rely on past experiences and conditioning to provide direction, and find it difficult to use—or even relate to—intuition.

56

Using the brain in this way tends to make Reds conservative in their thinking and behavior. Because of the rigidity of left-brain functioning, this color tends to be strong-minded, stubborn, straightforward, and aggressive and prefers predictability rather than spontaneity. There isn't room for chaos or the desire to speculate on abstract theories, which explains their strong need to control both people and their environment.

The Red personality is the most determined, hard-charging, controlling, aggressive, forceful, domineering, and intimidating of all the colors. They're not timid, nor are they wishy-washy. Whether it's driving a project or getting someone to do what they want, the Reds are always pushing. They also aren't the type to leave you guessing about what's on their mind—they'll always let you know, in no uncertain terms, what they think about you or how you're acting, whether you're doing what they want, or if you aren't meeting their expectations.

They'll never leave you guessing, but they *will* leave you in the dust if you move too slowly or are indecisive. Reds take charge of a situation and expect others to do the same. They aren't easily intimidated, nor are they hesitant to bulldoze their way through something or run over anything or anyone who gets in their way. The saying "Lead, follow, or get out of the way" best describes those in this color, especially once they make up their minds about what needs to be done or how to do it. Their perspective is that if others can't keep up or put up with their intensity, then stay out of the way.

Reds are the "just get it done" people, and they expect the same from everyone else. They pride themselves on their ability to manage time, be productive, and hit their deadlines. They have zero tolerance for those who are lazy or lack initiative or don't follow through on their commitments. If

Reds make a commitment to you, from their perspective it's cast in concrete; conversely, if you promise them something, that's also set in stone. It doesn't make any difference to them if your circumstances change. They see that as your problem, not theirs.

Reds are also very much the "it's all about me" people. They're demanding, impatient, self-centered, and self-serving and can be brutally honest in expressing what they're thinking. Because of their logical and sensible nature, they can appear to be insensitive to the other colors. This really isn't the case, especially from the Reds' perspective. It's just that they don't place the same value on emotions that some of the other personalities do. Consequently, they don't see the need for expressing their own feelings (other than anger), nor do they think it's necessary for others to do so.

For Reds, emotions are distractions and hindrances that impede progress and the problem-solving process. They don't understand why people can't just get over it when their feelings are hurt. Folks in this color are more interested in achieving their objectives than winning popularity contests. If getting what they want and need forces them to step on a few toes, then that's just the way it goes. They figure that it's the other person's problem anyway, so let them deal with it. As a matter of fact, Reds see emotional outbursts as signs of weakness, being out of control, and the inability to manage behavior.

These people aren't very good when it comes to saying "I'm sorry" or having to admit that they're wrong. If Reds do find themselves in a position where they've made a mistake or said something hurtful, they'll usually attribute it to just being a minor misunderstanding rather than a big problem. They aren't driven by guilt, nor do they find it necessary to explain themselves. Their aggressive, controlling nature and domineering approach can wear people down, especially the colors that tend to relate and interact emotionally.

Don't worry about needing to coax a Red to establish their place in a hierarchy. They're born leaders who tend to run both their homes and their work environments in a strict, regimented, organized, and straightforward manner. As a result, some of the other personalities look to them to take charge and are more than happy letting them make the decisions and accept the responsibility for what happens.

Reds know what they want: to have things their way. They're stubborn and expect that others won't question their decisions or their authority. They're confident and aren't concerned with how other people feel about them, because the need to be liked isn't what drives their behavior, nor is it a criterion they use to measure their success. The only data Reds place value on are results; everything is measured against the bottom line. It makes no difference how hard someone tries or how much effort they expend—if the results aren't there, then the person failed. As one Red put it in a workshop I gave: "Effort isn't something you can take to the bank."

The Reds' need for control is primarily driven by their fear of being blindsided or caught off guard. They don't like surprises, so to ensure that they feel safe, they'll tend to over-compensate by micromanaging and displaying demanding and domineering behavior. This affects their ability to delegate, because until they're absolutely sure that someone can be trusted to get the job done correctly and on time, they'd rather do it themselves. However, when Reds find people they can rely on, it isn't unlike them to bury these folks with all the tasks that they personally don't want to do. Yet ironically, they'll still assume the position of power just because they can't let go completely.

Reds enjoy a good fight and love the smell of victory. They're fierce competitors and see a contest as one of the joys of life, approaching any such situation with enthusiasm and vigor. However, they have a difficult time recognizing when it's time to stop and move on to something else. Consequently, they'll push themselves beyond what's healthy for their bodies or their self-esteem. They view themselves as survivalists, and if winning is the name of the game, then it's their job to come out on top—no matter what it takes to do so. Their motto is "Never give up! Damn the torpedoes, and full speed ahead!" They can be stubborn and intimidating and will move forward with brute strength if they think that's what it takes to be the victor. If you're a personality color who doesn't deal well with confrontation, then you might want to reconsider putting yourself in a competitive situation with a Red.

These people are driven by objectives. They enjoy the process of setting goals and putting together their action plan—gathering all pertinent information, evaluating what has worked before and what hasn't, eliminating questionable options, creating a master plan, setting a timeline, and then driving themselves and other people to ensure that everything happens in the way it should. Failure isn't an option for Reds, so they'll take whatever action is needed to get what they want, whether it's assuming an aggressive posture or using intimidation. They'll harness their self-discipline skills and commit the time and resources needed, then buckle down and stick to the program.

Reds are successful because there's no doubt in their mind that they'll succeed. If it requires hard work, sticking with a regimen, managing details, and refusing to follow the path of least resistance, this color wins, hands down. Their personal standards include exceeding other people's expectations, setting the bar high enough to separate themselves from everyone else, respecting authority, being loyal, and not giving up when the going gets tough. Their competitive nature helps them achieve these goals.

Learning Style

The learning-style sequence for the Red is *auditory, conceptual, visual,* and *kinesthetic.* This reveals that the Red begins acquiring knowledge externally, based on what they hear. If that makes sense to them—meaning that it creates understanding and gives them the information the way they need—then they move internally and create a mental picture of what they heard, after which they proceed to the other modes.

However, if what they hear is vague—if it isn't specific enough or clearly stated—they can't move forward in the learning process. The result is that they'll fall back on their previous knowledge, and consequently will base their solutions on what's familiar. They can't create a new mental picture or come up with a fresh concept, so they'll stick with what's safe.

As students, whether in school or in business, Reds perceive the information they hear concretely and take it literally. They discover things by listening and putting the data into their own words. They value clarification and also learn through direct experience, meaning that they want to be involved in the process and the outcome.

Reds match current information with past performance to see if what they need to know has validity. If it does, they're open and receptive; if it doesn't, they dismiss their need to stay involved and shut down. Those in this color have a limited tolerance for the theoretical, speculation, and ambiguity. They need details and facts rather than the subjective opinions of other people. They learn mostly through trial and error, and their focus is primarily directed toward perfecting old skills.

Reds are industrious and thorough in their desire to learn. Like everything else in life, they approach studying from a take-charge perspective. They work hard at figuring things out and set high standards for both themselves and others. If what they're working on is difficult, they'll buckle down and stick with it until they get it done right. They tend to become anxious when under pressure and are frustrated if they can't find the information or directions they need. Reds expect the learning process to produce results and don't see any value in taking the time to learn something new if it doesn't have a practical application.

Here are some noteworthy qualities of the Red learning style:

Strength:	Practical applications of ideas
Learn by:	Factual information gathered through listening
Skill:	Work hard to make their organization productive
Weakness:	Make unilateral decisions because they believe that their decisions are always right
Motivation to learn:	Answer the question "How"— How does this work? How should it be done? How can we make it more efficient?

Learning Objective:	Gain a better understanding and produce solutions to problems
Application:	Ask them to get involved in a project. Tell them specifically what you need from them: Clearly identify the problem, give them a deadline, let them think about it, and send them a memo restating the problem and desired outcome. Then stay out of their way. They'll come to you if they need more information.

Management Style

Reds tend to follow traditional management proce-dures—after all, these things have worked for a long time, so why change? These people are tenacious, dogmatic, and strong-minded and pride themselves on producing results. They're heavy-handed managers who believe in pushing hard to get what they want. They have a sense of what's right and how things should be done and aren't hesitant to share their thoughts or opinions with others, running a tight ship and demanding that others comply with their rules.

They expect people to go above and beyond the call of duty and become disappointed when someone doesn't. Reds see such behavior as letting the team down and smack-ing of irresponsibility. Since these managers are dedicated to their jobs, they expect their employees to be equally involved and to do whatever it takes and put in whatever time is necessary to meet any and all objectives.

While Reds' strengths lie in their ability to get others to execute tasks and produce results, they tend to fall short in their interpersonal skills. Their tendency is to be critical and judgmental and to deal with people in an assertive and direct manner. They expect everyone to follow through on their commitments and hit their goals and will push to see that this occurs.

Reds become impatient with those who are emotional, always have excuses, lack common sense, aren't prepared, are disorganized, or aren't motivated to succeed. They can be insensitive, cold, and even hard-hearted when dealing with someone they perceive has let them down, and they have no trouble dismissing anyone who doesn't meet their approval.

Red managers believe that their people must earn their respect and prove themselves and that the only way to do so is through performance. Since those in this color set high standards for themselves, they expect others to perform to those levels, meaning that anything less than 100 percent doesn't count. The most common complaints about Red managers are their intolerance of people's idiosyncrasies and the fact that they're never satisfied—the minute one goal is reached, they set the bar higher.

Working for a Red is a good news/bad news situation. The upside is that if you meet or exceed their expectations, they'll reward you, sometimes with more responsibility. The drawback is that if you fall short, you won't stay a part of their team. This color is binary—you're either in or you're out. When a person displays the desire to succeed, the Reds move into their mentor modes and teach the basic fundamentals of what it takes to be successful—hard work, setting goals, taking control of the situation, never losing sight of the objective, persevering even when the going gets tough, and exceeding expectations.

As managers, Reds are action driven, bottom-line motivated, and the movers and shakers in any organization. Their greatest assets include their loyalty; the ability to find the most expedient way to get things done with the least amount of resources; their determination; and how they confidently move from point A to point B, never wavering in commitment or follow-through.

They don't mind redundancy—in fact, they prefer it and are masters at managing mundane details. Reds aren't afraid to roll up their sleeves and become hands-on managers if that's what's required. They're also keen observers. Consequently, they can spot trouble even before it bubbles to the surface. In addition, they're respectful of authority and skillful at working the chain of command to make their solutions and suggestions heard.

Reds can be the voice of reason when they think that the choices being made are the wrong ones, and they'll take an adversarial role if they believe that things haven't been thought through completely. Since the people in this color are ruled by their head, they see it as their responsibility to stop others from making mistakes or taking risks that could jeopardize their finances, careers, family, or future. As a matter of fact, it's incomprehensible to Reds that people would even consider acting on their intuition, a whim, an urge, or the speculations of others without fully investigating the legitimacy of the situation and then rationally weighing the pros and cons. From this color's perspective, that's just good common sense . . . and if people do otherwise, then they deserve what they get.

The Reds' fear of being unprepared is what drives their desire for control and accountability. As managers, they want reports showing what their employees are doing, who they're talking to, where they've been, where they're going, and what steps they're taking to ensure that the job will be done right and on time. These supervisors follow standard operating procedures, and if people play by their rules and keep them in the loop, they'll be less inclined to micromanage.

Their leadership style is characterized by their bullish aggressiveness to win and their unwillingness to give up. They're intense, singularly focused, hard-charging, intimidating, forceful, and unrelenting in pushing to get what they want. They enjoy playing the game and putting together a winning strategy that will send them to the top and keep them there. They're confident and sell themselves well, using facts and past experiences to support their ideas and plans.

Reds can also take advantage of other people's vulnerabilities if that's what it takes to succeed. They'll actively solicit other perspectives as a way to get a handle on what's happening and then use that information to develop their plan. They're good at identifying problems and turning those challenges into opportunities for themselves to increase their power, status, and wealth. They pride themselves on their ability to make things happen and garner the cooperation of other people. They're social and charismatic when they need something, but impatient and inconsiderate when someone else is asking for favors.

As leaders, they're highly selective of who will ride the wave of success with them. Consequently, they'll tend to surround themselves with people who are loyal, steadfast, and trustworthy. Reds are bold, authoritarian leaders who are used to getting what they want.

Communication Style

Communication isn't one of the Red's greatest virtues, nor is this color very tolerant or patient with the process, because it requires both listening and talking. Whether introverted or extroverted, these people are more interested in the latter. In any conversation, they're just waiting for the opportunity to give advice and tell other people how to do things.

However, there are a few exceptions: They'll be open to listening to what you have to say if it leads to what they want, and they're also motivated to find out what they need to know. You may catch their attention if you're discussing something that interests them or it sounds like you know what you're talking about. Do not, however, misinterpret their focus as meaning that they agree with what you're saying, because that might not be the case. They'll listen as a means of identifying what position you're taking, and then they'll share their take on things—which will usually be the opposite of yours, as they enjoy taking an opposing role and playing devil's advocate.

It also helps to keep in mind that listening skills tend to differ from one personality color to another. When it comes to Reds, most of the time when they appear to be listening they're actually thinking about the next thing they're going to share, and the minute they get their words formulated, they open up and out it comes—even if it means interrupting you. However, Reds don't see themselves as cutting you off, they just think they're trying to help you get back on track and ensuring that you have your facts straight.

Small talk, unfounded speculation, or discussions dealing with emotional issues are irritating and a waste of time from a Red's perspective, as are both chitchat that seems to go nowhere and brainstorming sessions. They're not interested in engaging in meetings where there isn't an objective or some sort of action plan to be implemented. Reds see the conversation process as needing to serve a purpose, initiate an action, and be productive. They have no patience or interest in participating in conversations that ramble on about nothing or that rehash a situation over and over again. Reds want to talk about things that are practical, tangible, measurable, and centered on their own interests. The minute they decide a conversation isn't going where they think it should, they'll jump in and redirect it or get up and leave the room. It seems that their need to be in control even applies to the communication process.

Reds enjoy conversations that focus on making things happen and on activities involving planning. They like mapping out vacations, their future, and how to manage their finances; deciding when to buy a new car or house or when to retire; or figuring out what they'll do when they finally stop working. They're not interested in sitting around gossiping or talking about the same old problems.

Even though Reds want to be included in the discussion, don't expect them to openly volunteer information. You'll probably have to pull things out of them or wait until you're having dinner with friends to find out what's really happening in their lives. The reason Reds share so openly with friends is because they don't feel they have to be accountable to them in the same way that they are to their loved ones. Consequently, they'll open up and you'll get the entire scoop about what's going on.

Reds are blunt, straightforward, frank, and matter-of-fact in their communication style. Their hallmark is telling it like it is, and they don't mince words or worry whether they'll step on toes or hurt someone's feelings in the process. When something you're doing is bothering them, or if they're unhappy with you, they'll tell you. They won't leave you guessing about what's going on.

This color also interprets things literally, which means that they'll believe and act on what they hear. Once spoken, words become cast in concrete, and Reds will hold you to the commitments you make. So if you're going to use Reds as sounding boards, be sure to tell them that's what you're doing. Otherwise, they'll quickly jump in and begin to solve your problems—whether you have any or not. Worse yet, they may start giving you advice on how you should handle a situation or person before you've even had time to think about it. The real clincher in conversations where you're just ruminating on things is that they'll expect you to follow through on the advice they give you, even though that's not what you wanted or needed.

Teamwork Style

Reds bring a sense of direction, stability, and leadership to the team. They enjoy being an integral part of a development and implementation process and seek to make a positive contribution. They're cooperative team players and are willing to jump in and take action, doing whatever is necessary to get the job finished. They're responsible and decisive and are at their best when managing people's activities and the details surrounding a project or task. They're sensible and reasonable, so they deal with issues objectively rather than personally. This ability allows them to deal with others in a direct manner and helps keep everyone focused on the tasks at hand, thus minimizing the potential for personality conflicts.

Reds have strong opinions about how things should be done and are quick to point out why suggestions won't work or when someone makes a mistake. They expect the team to follow their lead without question. They're quick to make decisions once they think they understand the problem and are even quicker in implementing the necessary steps needed to make the issue go away. However, there's a risk in their quick decision-making style: If they take action based on other people's opinions rather than getting the necessary facts, they can lead everyone astray.

Their organizational skills and their predictability are a real plus. You can always count on Reds to be consistent in both their opinions and their behavior. Flighty, indecisive, unpredictable, or fickle, they're not.

This color expects people to work together and not be focused on individual needs. If these managers think that others aren't contributing to the success of the group or are engaged in self-serving behavior, they'll swiftly and aggressively call them on it and remind them of their place and responsibilities. They're outspoken advocates of rules and expect others to abide by those rules without question.

Reds are steadfast and methodical in how they work toward objectives and expect the same from others. They see teamwork as everyone being on the same page, marching to the same drummer, keeping an eye on the prize, and doing whatever it takes to ensure the desired results. If their subordinates follow these steps, everything moves forward smoothly. However, when people don't carry their weight or contribute their fair share, the Reds will write them off and will align themselves with those who understand what they think working together really means.

Should this happen, it doesn't take long for the rejected individuals to recognize that they're no longer viewed as part of the team. Remember, Reds aren't known for their subtlety.

They believe that everything should be out in the open—no hidden agendas. They like:

- Leadership roles
- Predictable work environments
- Decisive action plans
- Competitive situations
- Group participation
- Challenging tasks
- An overall organizational plan

Overview of the Red Personality

Basic Needs:

- Control of people and their environment
- Sticking with what's familiar and tried-and-true
- Structure and order
- Matter-of-fact relationships
- Immediate and tangible rewards as recognition of a job well done
- Minimal change
- Routine and a life that's predictable

Strengths:

- Organizational skills
- No-nonsense approach
- Take-charge attitude
- Responsible, dependable, and reliable
- Steadfast and predictable
- Competitive and strong willed
- Hardworking, resourceful, and self-reliant
- Sensible, practical, and pragmatic

What They Value:
- Authority
- Control
- Tradition
- Results
- Personal achievements
- Belonging and being an integral part of a group
- Security

Behavioral Motivations:
- Power
- Status
- Wealth
- Recognition

Limitations:
- Self-serving focus ("It's all about me")
- Need to be always right
- Demanding and insensitive
- Resistant to change
- Critical and judgmental
- Dogmatic and rigid
- Become overwhelmed with too many problems
- Anger easily

Blind Spots:
- Focus more on the tasks at hand and their responsibilities than on the needs of people
- Choose not to acknowledge when they're wrong or admit to inadequacies because of fear of appearing vulnerable or losing control

- Tell others what they should and shouldn't do and how they should act
- Lack patience with people who don't produce results or follow through on commitments
- See it as being helpful to point out other people's inadequacies, whether others think it's constructive or not
- Become impatient with tasks and objectives that take too long; want quick fixes and immediate results
- Tend to dwell in the past rather than looking to the future
- Create chaos, turmoil, and conflict when they think they're losing their grip or appear out of control

Insecurities:
- Fear of losing what they've acquired
- Being emotionally vulnerable
- Financial devastation

Room for Improvement:
- Developing communication skills (specifically, listening)
- Increasing emotional sensitivity to other people's needs
- Being receptive to new ideas and open to change
- Letting go of the need to always be right
- Learning to manage anger
- Remembering that people do things for their own reasons
- Needing to always win
- Showing appreciation

Authority Relationships:

- Respect the chain of command and work effectively within it
- Try hard to earn respect of superiors
- Want face-to-face supervision and involvement
- Need to know they're supported
- Look to superiors for guidance and direction

Relationships with Peers:

- Forceful and dominant
- Critical
- Opinionated
- Rarely provide feedback
- Will only involve themselves with peers they respect or whom they think can be an ally to their success
- Competitive
- Difficulty delegating authority

Irritations:

- People wasting their time
- Those who don't follow through on commitments
- Emotional outbursts and too much sentimentalism
- Being told how to work and do something
- Questioning them or their decisions
- Anyone who breaks the rules they choose to observe

How They Irritate Others:

- Bossing people around and needing to always be right
- Being too rigid
- Not listening and jumping to conclusions
- Being impatient
- Making unilateral decisions
- Measuring success only by the bottom line and not placing value on effort
- Dismissing other people's perceptions and ignoring their needs
- Telling and yelling rather than listening
- Unwillingness to go with the flow

What Causes Stress:

- Dealing with other people's problems
- Feeling out of control
- Objectives not being met
- Having to wait for others
- Incompetence, inefficiency, and irrational behavior
- Ambiguity in what the tasks are or how performance will be measured

What Reds Need to Function Effectively:

- A stable, secure work environment where they're not dealing with a lot of organizational change
- Challenges that allow them to develop action plans and utilize their organizational skills
- Well-defined tasks and responsibilities and clearly stated standards of measurement
- A sense of direction, a timeline, and an understanding of their roles

- Superiors and peers who express appreciation for what they bring to the group
- Routine, redundancy, and predictability

When Dealing with Reds, Do . . .

- Be direct, straightforward, and brief.
- State the facts and present issues logically.
- Clearly explain what needs to be done and what you need from them.
- Remain calm when communicating and avoid emotional outbursts.
- Approach them with confidence.
- Be prepared to back up your recommendations with facts and figures.
- Respond to their needs and express your appreciation for their hard work.
- Offer them leadership opportunities and support with financial incentives.
- Demand their attention and work to earn their respect.
- Be productive and efficient, and keep them updated on task or project status.
- Respect their need to do things their way and make their own decisions.
- Be punctual and considerate of their time.
- Respect their need for routine and redundancy.

When Dealing with Reds, Don't . . .

- Rehash a decision that's already been made or an issue that's settled. They perceive this as a total waste of time and energy.

- Give them ultimatums.

- Exaggerate or share your opinions.

- Put yourself in a power struggle with them— you'll lose.

- Expect them to say "I'm sorry" or "I made a mistake."

- Ask them to compromise their beliefs.

- Anticipate that they'll change without digging in their heels. Just present the idea and let them mull it over until they think it's their idea—then it will be acceptable.

- Embarrass them or point out their insecurities in front of other people.

- Attack them personally. The reaction you get won't be pleasant, and then they'll pout.

- Commit their time without first checking with them.

- Assume that they know what you need. Just tell them.

- Wait for them to ask you what you think or solicit your opinions.

- Use an authoritarian approach or try to one-up them. Their competitive nature will kick into high gear, and what should be a cooperative effort will become a battle of wills.

The Red World:
*Take care of the molehills, and
the mountains will take care of themselves.*

※ ※ ※

CHAPTER FIVE

The Orange Personality:
It's All about Relationships

The information in this chapter is intended to offer a comprehensive overview of the Orange personality that can be used as a reference guide. It's presented from a pragmatic perspective for dealing with superiors, interacting with peers, or supervising subordinates. It's intended to be both useful and directly applicable. I've addressed the most relevant aspects of the Orange's behavioral patterns and neurology—including personality, learning, management, communication, and teamwork styles—and have concluded with a brief overview that can be easily accessed when a situation doesn't warrant a lengthy explanation.

Oranges at a Glance

Oranges are unassuming, devoted, considerate, warm, friendly, and truly interested in the needs of others. Their innermost desire is to help people and to provide a stable, secure, predictable, and safe work environment. They want to make a difference in others' lives and assist them in any way possible to succeed and to accomplish their goals. Harmony and cooperation are their core themes because they dislike conflict and will do anything to avoid it. Their desire to please and lend a hand will often find them taking on too much or working long hours. This can be a problem, as they're constantly trying to juggle work and home responsibilities.

Those of this color are good workers who will do whatever's required to please the boss. They take direction well and maintain a positive attitude. Oranges thrive on social interaction and consider their peers and employees to be their extended family, caring for them as if they were close relations.

Their needs are those of the group. Consequently, they'll include everyone in any decision-making process that will somehow impact them. They get personal satisfaction when working on the fulfillment of directives and goals.

Oranges form relationships easily and work hard to keep these connections a top priority, meaning that they'll think about you, do thoughtful things, listen, worry about you, and even make sacrifices if it means that they can help. They're completely committed to others and will remain so through the good times and the bad times. In other words, you can always count on them to be there.

These folks are frequently comfortable being in positions of less visible leadership, since they see their roles as being more supportive. They're respectful of authority, loyal, noncompetitive, and have little need to be in the limelight or share in the credit or glory. In fact, they prefer it that way, because being the center of attention is uncomfortable to them.

Oranges are thorough, competent, efficient, dependable, reliable, detail oriented, and good at what they do. They set high standards for themselves and have a strong work ethic. They're conscientious about their obligations and responsibilities, so it's easy for other people, especially their bosses, to rely heavily upon them to handle unwanted tasks. These attentive and active listeners are also often used as sounding boards by other colors. Their ability to manage tasks and work well with people makes them valuable assets to any organization.

Oranges, like Reds, enjoy routine, structure, and well-defined job responsibilities. Knowing what they need to do and how they'll be evaluated makes it easier for them to perform and minimizes their tendency to fret about what's expected of them. Lowering anxiety is vitally important to the health and well-being of Oranges, as they are perennial worriers.

Because of their tendency to take on a supportive role, they'll often find it difficult to take advantage of opportunities for their own advancement. Rather than compete or take an aggressive posture, they'll hold back until someone approaches them and makes an offer.

Ten Predictable Behavioral Traits of the Orange Personality

Here are ten of the most predictable and observable behavioral traits of Oranges. Each one helps them fulfill their innermost desire: to help and take care of other people. Although other personality colors may display what appears to be similar behaviors, an Orange will demonstrate them more consistently and frequently.

1. Cooperative. Oranges are cooperative and respectful of authority. They function best in environments where teamwork is encouraged and people are sensitive to the feelings and needs of others. They're careful to maintain a courteous, polite, and restrained demeanor and will do whatever it takes to create mutually satisfying relationships where everyone's needs are met. They're easygoing, adaptable, and willing to pitch in when needed.

2. Social. Oranges would rather be with others than be alone. They're social and enjoy spending time with those they care about. Their idea of a good time is being involved in activities where people can enjoy each other's company, learn more about each other's likes and dislikes, and share in the bonds of friendship. Whether it's a social lunch or a major business event, Oranges will see to it that everybody feels welcome, is well cared for and comfortable, and is made to feel special.

3. Generous. Oranges' generosity and emotional sensitivity are their greatest contributions to other personality colors. They give freely of their time and resources and aren't the type to wait to be asked to help—they'll just step in. Their unselfish nature motivates them to lend a hand to anyone who needs it, from family members and friends to total strangers. Oranges really would give someone the shirt off their back if they felt it could help or if it was really needed. They do such things without any expectations other than being appreciated and acknowledged.

4. Caring. Oranges are genuinely concerned about the emotional well-being of others. They're thoughtful and caring and always act from the heart. These individuals understand the need to have someone who truly cares and whom others can count on, so they show how they feel through sincere actions and outreach. Since their innermost desire is to be of service to humankind, they're interested in seeing that everyone is treated with respect and dignity. They want to ensure that people are appreciated for their uniqueness and their contributions.

5. Emotional. Emotions rule the Oranges' lives and drive their behavior. They're so emotionally sensitive that it's easy for them to get hurt over the slightest things. As a result, they can tell when others are upset or having a difficult time. This trait can be a double-edged sword—on the one hand it helps them "take the pulse" of a situation to discover what's really going on around them, but on the other hand, it distresses them to see others suffer. People know that if they ever need to talk something through, Oranges will always be there for them.

6. Traditional. Those in this group are traditionalists and don't waver in their perceptions of how people should be treated. They have strong moral values, which they expect others to share. It's their traditional nature that creates their need to follow well-established policies and support the needs of an organization. Other personality colors look to Oranges for security and stability in relationships and know they'll always provide an organized and conflict-free environment. People count on Oranges to offer support and see them as the being the backbone of any company.

7. Apprehensive. Oranges have a tendency to continually be looking over their shoulders, as if waiting for the next shoe to drop, especially when things are going well. Since they're worriers, they often live with ongoing anxiety, anticipating that something bad is going to happen. Oranges don't like to be caught off guard, so their apprehensive nature is one way for them stay alert and ensure they won't be blindsided. They're forever second-guessing themselves and fretting about things they have no control over.

8. Moody. While trying to always appear positive, Oranges are actually moody and pensive. Their state of mind is directly connected to how they're feeling about their relationships and jobs and whether they're feeling appreciated or if people are taking advantage of them. They're emotionally binary, meaning that life is either good or bad: They're happy or sad, optimistic or pessimistic, upbeat or miserable. When Oranges are feeling positive, everything is wonderful and their outlook is bright. When they're not feeling so great, everything is a problem, and they're very difficult to be around.

9. Devoted. Oranges are devoted, committed, and dedicated. Their loyalty to those they care about is so strong that they'll stand by them through thick and thin—no matter how unpleasant or how painful the experience. It isn't uncommon for Oranges to take on other people's emotional burdens if they believe that doing so can somehow lighten the load.

10. Guilt-ridden. Guilt weighs heavily on Oranges' shoulders, so it's difficult for them to ask for help or bother anyone with their problems. They're concerned that if they make requests, other people might have to do things they don't want to. They feel bad when they make errors, when they buy something expensive for themselves, or when they think that they've hurt someone's feelings. Oranges see it as their role to be peacemakers and create an environment where everyone gets along. When they're unable to do so, they feel guilty and believe they've let everyone down.

Personality Style

ORANGE PERSONALITY

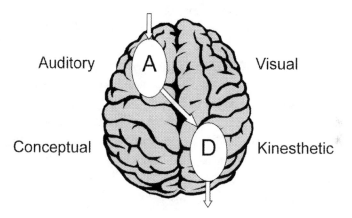

Auditory A Visual

Conceptual D Kinesthetic

The Orange personality quadrant combination is A and D, which means that they begin gathering information with the left brain and then move to the right brain to make decisions. This neurological crossover takes time and can be challenging, because on the left side, the data must make sense and has to be approached methodically; while on the right, things have to be mulled over emotionally and then judged as good or bad before anything can happen. If neither side gets what it needs, Oranges become emotionally overwhelmed and are prone to indecision.

When Oranges are pressed to make a choice before both quadrants can get what they need, they experience frustration, agitation, and irritation and retreat inward. Their intention in doing so is to avoid conflict and hope that the problem will just go away without their involvement.

Emotional feedback is critical for people in this color because it helps them evaluate how their actions are going to affect others. Because of the emotional sensitivity from the right decision-making quadrant, they don't want to do anything that's going to have a negative impact. Oranges are binary in their emotional evaluations—information is right or wrong, the impact of their decision is good or bad, and experiences are pleasant or unpleasant. There are no gray areas in their neurology; things are never just okay or mediocre.

Oranges are the moodiest and most emotional of all the personalities. Helping others and seeing that their needs are met is what adds meaning to the lives of those in this color; it gives them a sense of belonging and purpose. Their sensitivity is expressed in their sympathetic and compassionate nature. When Oranges ask you how you're feeling, they're not just being courteous—they're really interested. Asking this question accomplishes two things:

1. It allows them to take your emotional pulse to see if you're okay or distressed.

2. It lets them evaluate the environment to get a sense of whether it's friendly or charged with conflict.

Because of their sensitivity, Oranges may actually experience what people are feeling. As a result, they have a very strong need to comfort others, and this outreach is sincere and genuine. These folks aren't fair-weather friends. They'll be there when you're feeling down, in need of help, overwhelmed, and feel like your world is crumbling all around you, as well as when things are going well. In other words, they'll share the good times and the bad. They'll always offer support and be there to listen.

Oranges are the ultimate caretakers: devoted, committed, loyal, and self-sacrificing. In this respect, Oranges' families rank at the top of the list; then come friends, co-workers, church members, and their community. Looking out for themselves and their own needs is down at the bottom.

If you were to ask Oranges what they do for themselves, the common response would be "When?" accompanied by a look that seems to question why you'd ask such a silly thing. These people will tell you that they don't have any time for themselves because their lives are so centered around juggling the demands of family, work, and social activities that by the time they do get around to trying to do something for themselves, they're either too tired or someone else needs something. While this may seem incomprehensible to other personality colors, Oranges see it as their responsibility to accommodate those they care about and to be available whenever they're needed.

It always surprises Oranges and even disappoints them when the sensitivity, caring, courtesy, and outreach they instinctively extend to others isn't reciprocated. Members of this color expect everybody they care for to be there for them and return the same sensitivity and understanding—without having to be asked. When they don't receive the same emotional nurturing that they provide to others, Oranges feel taken advantage of, unloved, unsupported, betrayed, and abandoned. They experience deep pain because they can't understand why others don't care for them, or what they've done so wrong that people don't reach out to them.

However, one of the reasons why Oranges don't get what they want and need is that they don't ask for it. They assume that because they do thoughtful things, other people will instinctively and automatically want to do the same. Another cause for a shortage of emotional warm fuzzies is that when someone does express their appreciation, Oranges quickly dismiss their actions as no big deal; say, "No problem"; or imply that it isn't necessary to thank them. Unfortunately, the other personality colors take this at face value. Plus, Oranges make taking care of people look so effortless that everyone tends to take what they do for granted.

Consequently, others forget to show appreciation and reach out to them when they're in need of a little tender loving care. They forget to acknowledge how Oranges' concerned and supportive natures add significantly to the quality of their lives. These people don't require a lot of praise or acknowledgment for what they do; they just need to hear how much what they do is appreciated every so often. Then their willingness to care for others will remain foremost in their minds.

Oranges need stability and feel the most secure when they're involved in predictable relationships, whether at work or in their personal lives. They feel safe in these situations because they measure their self-worth and value through the contributions they make to others; how they feel about themselves is directly tied to the quality of their interactions. When they feel good about the relationship and are valued and appreciated, they're happy and have pleasant dispositions. They're enjoyable to be around and doing things for others is easy. On the other hand, if they aren't feeling good about how things are going with the people they know, then they're moody and unapproachable, their outlook on life is negative, their disposition is sour, and their behavior will alternate between being passive and aggressive—one minute they're not speaking to you, and the next minute you wish they weren't.

There's an old saying, "Ain't Mama happy, ain't nobody happy." This can apply to both male and females. Since who they are and how they feel about themselves is so tied to their relationships, they'll often identify themselves through others—that is, it isn't unusual to hear Oranges say, "I work for so-and-so," or "I'm in so-and-so's department." It's almost as if they lose their personal identity and take on that of their boss or their responsibilities.

Oranges don't deal well with conflict and have a difficult time functioning where there's constant tension, personality conflicts, and unresolved issues. Hostile and insensitive environments keep them emotionally off balance and undermine their ability to work. If they find themselves in a highly charged situation, they'll become submissive and overly compliant and withdraw rather than saying what they're feeling. They'll go into avoidance behavior until the tension subsides and things become friendly and emotionally stable again.

Oranges' nature is to overextend themselves as a means of pleasing others and gaining their approval. They'll overcompensate by working hard to meet people's expectations. When they do go beyond the call of duty and it isn't recognized or appreciated, they'll become frustrated, resentful, angry, and unforgiving. Their behavior shifts from being compliant and engaging to domineering, demanding, and nitpicky.

Unlike Reds, who will vent their anger and frustration and then move on, Oranges will suppress their emotions until they reach the point where they can't keep them bottled up any longer. When this happens, there won't be any doubt that they've had all they can take. Their outburst will be so explosive that it will leave you gasping. You'll stand there wondering how to get out of their way and asking yourself what just happened. Their release of pent-up emotions can be so venomous and spiteful that it leaves others completely stunned.

There are ways to prevent this; however, it means heightening your sensitivity to their personal needs, telling them on a regular basis how much you appreciate all they do for you, and making the time to listen so that they can share how they're feeling. This isn't really much to ask for, considering what they do for everyone else.

The world of Oranges is driven by their emotions, reactions, and interactions. Things are black or white when it comes to how they feel about something or someone. Their rigidity is the result of their use of emotional judgments in the decision-making process, which can make them difficult to work with or be around. Because they hide their feelings so well, it's hard to know their opinions or where they're coming from or to read them in any way. As a result, people have a difficult time trusting them, because what they say they feel on the surface may not actually be true deep inside. Oranges are good at putting up facades that tell others everything is fine when it really isn't. Their unpredictable nature can make them caring, sensitive, and giving one moment and critical, tense, and unforgiving the next.

One of the greatest challenges for Oranges is to manage their fears and insecurities. They're the true worriers of the personality world. They stress about anything and everything, and sometimes don't even know why they're anxious or what they're upset about. They fret about finances and job security, as well as whether something bad will happen, whether they're doing a good job, if they're doing everything they can, if they're doing the right thing, and whether they're acting appropriately. They'll even worry about what total strangers think. Oranges constantly live with the anxiety that people aren't going to like them, are going to become angry or mistreat them, or—worse yet—abandon them.

Guilt is another major problem. They tend to hang on to past hurts and feelings of shame longer than any other color. They allow this to influence how they act, as well as their self-esteem. It isn't unusual for Oranges, as adults, to still be struggling with guilt that was created when they were children.

Because this is such a natural part of the Oranges' emotional makeup, they often fail to recognize how it causes them to do things they really don't want to do and stay in relationships they'd rather leave. They fail to recognize how guilt distorts their perspective, turns their desire to care for others into an obligation, and takes away the warm feelings they're looking for when they put the needs of others before their own.

Oranges just want everyone to get along and see themselves as peacemakers. They pride themselves on their ability to promote cooperation and create environments where people can feel safe in sharing their concerns. Oranges are considerate, diplomatic, and respectful of others' opinions, even if they don't agree. They appreciate interactions where support and acceptance are the objectives and where everyone makes an effort to coexist in harmony.

They also value individuality and diversity and recognize how differences contribute positively to their relationships. Oranges are patient and tolerant of idiosyncrasies and will tend to overlook disagreeable behavior if it will help maintain peace. If pushed, however, they'll take a passive posture and go into avoidance behavior rather than creating a confrontation. From their perspective, it's easier to stay out of someone's way until things blow over than to run the risk of hurt feelings.

Learning Style

The learning style sequence for Oranges is *auditory, kinesthetic, visual,* and *conceptual,* which reveals that these people begin the process externally based on what they hear. However, unlike Reds (who share the same mode for gathering information but who can't move forward internally until they get the facts), Oranges quickly and instinctively transition into the kinesthetic mode, because this added sensory input allows them to internalize and personalize what they're hearing.

In doing so, they can apply their emotional decision-making style to determine whether to go into the visual mode or turn back and ask for more data. Kinesthetic (touch) refers to their need to write things down so that they can internalize them. By putting auditory input into their own written words, they're able to move into the visual mode (reading), where they're able to effectively use their observation skills to support what they heard. If all the data makes sense and feels right, they go into the conceptual mode to gain understanding and determine how to act on what they're discovering, in addition to finding personal value in the process.

Oranges learn best by listening to other people's stories, what someone has done to become successful, how people changed their lives, and others' problems. They like to find out what will enhance their relationships, and see the acquisition of knowledge as a way to share feelings and build bonds. Oranges are naturally curious and want to hear how others are going to apply what they're learning to their everyday lives. Consequently, they're attracted to acquiring skills that will improve the quality of their lives and teach them how to be more effective at working and communicating.

Oranges learn best in settings that are emotionally nurturing, where people can feel safe in sharing their concerns and there's a sincere desire to accommodate each individual's needs. The environment must also be conflict free for Oranges to be receptive and engage in the process. If they're concerned at all about being embarrassed or criticized in front of their peers, their interest in working—or, for that matter, in staying there at all—quickly diminishes. If things don't change, this can even make them sick.

They need to feel safe and secure and want the environment to give them the time they need to grasp what they're trying to figure out and let them ask questions. It's important for them to be able to proceed at their own pace because they see learning as a means of personal expression and an integral part of personal growth, rather than just the acquisition of knowledge.

Here are some noteworthy qualities of Oranges' learning style:

Strength:	Building relationships
Learn by:	Listening and social interaction
Skill:	Engaging people in cooperative efforts for the purpose of creating organizational team spirit
Weakness:	Overly sensitive and get their feelings hurt easily
Motivation to learn:	Answer the question "Why?"— "Why can't people just get along?" "Why don't people take

the time to care?" "Why are others so focused on themselves
rather than the needs of the
group?"

Learning objective: Apply what they learn to helping people and improving
relationships

Application: Ask them for their help and verbally acknowledge their ability to
work well with people, as well as
the things they do for you. Tell
them what you need and when
you expect the results. Assure
them that you'll be there to support their efforts and answer any
questions they may have.

Management Style

Oranges are always the first to ask, "What can I do?"
They see their role as being supportive and cooperative.
Their ability to manage details, deal with people issues,
and handle loose ends makes them highly desirable team
members. Their need to please and make others feel comfortable, coupled with their ability to anticipate the likes and
dislikes of other personalities, makes them responsive, caring
managers.

Oranges are administrative masters and good at overseeing and handling many tasks or projects at one time.
They function effectively and are most productive when
they understand objectives and deadlines and are good at

garnering assistance in order to see that the job not only gets done—it gets done right.

Oranges' management style is strongly characterized by their sensitivity to the feelings of those they supervise. They're demanding perfectionists in setting their personal standards, but generally accepting in setting lesser standards for others. This nondirective approach makes them highly regarded by those reporting to them, along with the fact that they primarily operate through survey and consent.

Their philosophy is that those doing the jobs know best what's working and what isn't, and their responsibility as a manager is to support the good and correct everything else. As a result, they invest significant amounts of their time questioning those responsible for producing results for the organization. This engenders a family-like environment where people have a sense of importance in their contribution to the company's goals.

Oranges are tolerant, friendly, encouraging, and compassionate toward their staff. They see their role as a combination of counselor, teacher, and personal coach as they assist people in accomplishing their goals and achieving the success they desire. These managers take great pride in their team's accomplishments and will sing their praises to others. They're quick to express their appreciation and gratitude for a job well done and will go above and beyond the call of duty to make the work environment pleasant and rewarding. They're eager to provide whatever their group needs; they genuinely care and will maintain an open-door policy just to ensure that they're always available if someone needs them. They'll even encourage their people to call them at home or on the weekends if they need to talk.

While being sensitive feeds the Oranges' emotional need to take care of others, they struggle with many aspects of the responsibilities associated with managing. To begin with, they tend to worry too much about what their staff thinks of them, and thus have difficulty asserting themselves in conflicts. They also have difficulty delegating responsibility because of their need to be liked, and many times will find themselves being pushed around by a stronger, more aggressive personality. In addition, they have trouble with criticism and will personalize and internalize it—sometimes to the point of getting into a state of depression.

Finally, the toughest tasks for Oranges are disciplining and releasing workers, since they become bonded so tightly to their professional "family." In lieu of dealing with substandard performers in a straightforward fashion, they may choose to create improvement programs, offer reassignments, or modify jobs so that the individuals can succeed. However, this may undermine their respect in the eyes of those workers' peers.

As task managers, Oranges are at their best. They're dependable, organized, methodical, and systematic and can always be counted on to produce results. They're serious in tackling projects and enjoy making things happen and finding solutions to people problems. Vagueness about what needs to be done creates stress for Oranges and impacts their attitude and their productivity. They work in an action-oriented way, rallying the troops together to get the job done. They're good at time management and have a keen sense of how long things will really take, so they plan and pace themselves and their people accordingly.

When focused or pressed, Oranges become impatient and moody. This can be confusing to subordinates, because on the one hand Orange bosses are always telling them, "I'm here for you," but when people do step forward and the managers are in the middle of a task or project, they may get a cool reception.

Oranges are frequently described by the phrase "management by walking around," which refers to those who spend time outside their offices interacting with and listening to their people and the customer's needs. They're the least heavy-handed of all four personality types and—when in the right position—the most highly revered managers of all.

Their leadership style is strongly characterized by their desire to guide by example, meaning that they create the environment they want in order to be successful—one that's supportive, nurturing, and sensitive, where people have the opportunity to demonstrate their skills and produce not just adequate, but outstanding results. They're masterful at harnessing potential and building team support. Oranges are purposeful and dedicated and see it as their personal responsibility to inspire and motivate people to move beyond their self-perceived limitations. They're demanding leaders yet not aggressive. They truly want others to succeed, for they understand that this will bring them glory, too.

Loyal to the team and their causes, Oranges are strong advocates for what they believe in and will dedicate time, energy, and resources to help those who are in need. They believe in fairness and justice and loathe individual greed. They bring decency and strong moral values to the workplace, the home, and society. They believe their purpose in life is to care for others and to support them in their endeavors. As leaders, Oranges are highly committed to improving the quality of people's lives. They're sympathetic, listening with empathy, speaking passionately, and adding a special touch of sincere caring in their interactions.

These folks influence through doing rather than directing and are guided by their hearts rather than their heads. They adapt quickly and quietly, as they don't like to draw attention to themselves. They'd rather fly under the radar than be in the limelight.

Their leadership skills are best expressed by helping others, building cooperative relationships, and creating environments that promote harmony. They prefer being democratic rather than dictatorial leaders and are careful to solicit the input and feedback of other people before imposing their decisions on anyone. They make decisions by committee, meaning that they'll involve their associates, peers, and even staff members if the decisions being made will impact their lives.

Oranges measure their success as leaders by what they do for the good of others, not through the accumulation of wealth, power, or status. They achieve personal satisfaction from the deep, enduring, lifelong relationships they create and are more ambitious on behalf of others than they are for themselves.

Communication Style

Out of all aspects of human interaction, communication ranks the highest for Oranges. From their perspective, it's imperative to keep the lines open for relationships to continue, tasks to get done, and a cooperative and harmonious environment to be maintained. They believe that being able to share their concerns and how they feel becomes an integral part of the building and sustaining of mutually satisfying bonds. They view environments that devalue listening to people's concerns or that discourage the expression of feelings as being hostile and impossible to support.

Oranges think that the communication process should include some talking, but should mostly be about listening. Because they're naturally empathetic in this manner, they expect the same from others. They want to feel safe in discussing their concerns without fear of reprisal. Oranges long for people to actively listen, rather than thinking about what they're going to say next. They don't want to be interrupted or have their emotions, concerns, or suggestions dismissed. They want to be able to say what they really feel about something—not just what their bosses or peers want them to—and to share both positive and negative perspectives while feeling that they're being heard and taken seriously.

The worst thing that can happen to an Orange is to feel ignored or to have others say that they aren't interested in how they feel. Should this occur, they'll find it difficult to interact with these individuals and will begin the process of distancing and disconnecting from them. In this situation, it will be impossible for them to stay emotionally engaged in the relationship and maintain any degree of respect at all.

Oranges look for conversations that have emotional depth, not just the superficial rhetoric that serves as idle chatter. They use words that elicit an emotional reaction and tend to ask "why" questions. By doing so, they're able to get a sense of how someone feels, which is important since they aren't interested in wasting time talking about trivialities. They want to get right to the heart of matters and find out what's going on deep inside. They want to know what people are afraid of and why.

Oranges see the communication process as creating an intimate environment where everyone can safely and comfortably share their doubts, fears, and insecurities. They feel that if they encourage these kinds of conversations, there's less of a chance that they'll be caught off guard emotionally. Since their nature is to worry about what people think and to live in a constant state of low-grade anxiety, it's important for Oranges to be kept in the emotional loop conversationally. This is one way that they try to manage their stress and alleviate many of their fears. Being out of the loop conversationally is emotionally debilitating to them and increases their feelings of insecurity.

An ongoing issue for Oranges is continually feeling misunderstood. This baffles them because they perceive themselves as good communicators. And yes, they do a good job when it comes to telling others how they're feeling, but as for asking for what they need physically and emotionally . . . they tend to miss the mark.

Oranges don't feel they should have to ask. They just expect people to know what they need—which is the same as what they give to everyone else. When they finally do have to request something that seems obvious, it disappoints them and undermines how they feel about the people they're dealing with. They see these individuals as being insensitive, selfish, egocentric, unconcerned, uncaring, and only out for themselves. Having to ask someone to be sensitive to their needs makes them feel taken advantage of and puts them in a defensive posture, which breaks down the lines of communication and causes them to rethink whether these are people they want to interact with. And unless there are apologies or some kind of emotional outreach, in most cases Oranges will write these folks off and stop interacting with them. It doesn't take much to hurt their feelings.

Teamwork Style

Oranges are the embodiment of what teamwork is all about. Their strength lies in their ability to work well with others and create environments where everyone wants to get involved. They're concerned, listen with their hearts, and instinctively seek to maintain mutually satisfying relationships. They believe in camaraderie and value the differences each member brings to the group. They can always be counted on to be supportive and do whatever they can to ensure the success of the enterprise. They're eager to get involved, and once assigned a task, they'll see that it gets done.

Teamwork fosters the sharing of perceptions, ideas, and solutions while having fun. It supports harnessing the talents and strengths of everyone involved and seeing that their individual and collective needs are met. This is where Oranges excel across the board. They're pragmatic and realistic and aren't inclined to act hastily. They'd rather take the time to process the information emotionally and weigh the options before jumping to conclusions. Besides, they want the chance to discuss it with their teammates to get their perspectives.

Oranges are good at launching new ventures, overseeing their project-management responsibilities, and sticking with the plan until it's completed. Unlike some of the other personality colors who get bored with routine or who move on to another task before a current one is completed, Oranges remain focused on the job at hand and are unwavering in their commitment to produce results. Their steadfastness provides a sense of stability, predictability, and security for the team. They assume the role of facilitator and caretaker and are happiest when other people need them and value what they contribute. They like:

- Group interaction
- Participating in outreach activities
- Creating warm, friendly relationships
- Positive work environments
- Receiving appreciation for their organizational and administrative skills
- Getting clear direction from their supervisors
- Coordinating and planning activities and functions

Overview of the Orange Personality

Basic Needs:

- Conflict-free relationships
- Appreciation for what they give and all they do
- Other people who rely upon them
- A sense of purpose
- A supportive environment
- Financial security and stability
- Freedom to express their emotions
- The opportunity to care for other people's emotional well-being

Strengths:

- Organizational skills
- Stability and dependability
- Conscientiousness
- Sensitivity to others
- Listening skills
- Planning and execution
- Discipline with high personal standards
- Respect for authority

What They Value:

- Relationships
- Control
- Sincerity
- Predictability
- Tradition
- Devotion
- Loyalty

Behavioral Motivations:
- Being admired
- Being accepted
- Fostering dependency
- Security

Limitations:
- Feelings are easily hurt
- Inability to ask for what they need
- Self-righteous
- Self-deprecating
- High expectations of others' performances
- Unable to deal with sudden changes
- Easily discouraged
- Emotionally unpredictable
- Easily frustrated by lack of cooperation
- Low self-worth

Blind Spots:
- Suppressing emotions and opinions to avoid conflict
- Unwilling to face people issues that need to be addressed
- Overly sensitive to others' feedback
- Critical and judgmental when their feelings are hurt
- Overloading their schedules because of an inability to say no
- Controlling and demanding when people don't do what they want
- Allowing others to take advantage of their good nature because of their need to help

- Little tolerance for those who are aggressive and only concerned about themselves
- Misreading other people's intentions and internalizing events

Insecurities:
- Rejection
- Abandonment
- Doing something wrong
- Conflict

Room for Improvement:
- Learning to manage their emotions
- Asking for what they want and need and then accepting help
- Setting healthy boundaries and speaking up assertively
- Achieving a healthy work/home balance
- Learning to say no
- Speaking up if they feel they're being taken advantage of or mistreated

Authority Relationships:
- Respect and support authority
- Are loyal and dedicated, with a strong desire to please
- Follow rules and regulations
- Prefer agreeable and pleasant relationships
- Want delegated tasks to be clearly defined
- Need superiors to appreciate their contributions

Relationships with Peers:

- Easygoing, compliant, and cooperative
- Believe that direct orders offend people, and so prefer to suggest rather than tell
- Need to be valued
- Act nicely and fairly toward others, believing they'll receive the same consideration
- Treat people as equals and tend to be overly trusting
- Dependent on work associates to fill emotional needs

Irritations:

- Being treated impersonally and insensitively
- Expressing their emotions and concerns and then having them dismissed as hypersensitive outbursts
- Being taken for granted and feeling unappreciated
- Offering help and having people reject it
- Being put in situations where they have no control

How They Irritate Other People:

- Inability to take a stance; acting wishy-washy
- Emotional outbursts
- Martyrdom and sanctimonious behavior
- Playing "poor me," brooding, and pouting
- Moralistic and illogical
- Stubborn and unrealistic

What Causes Stress:

- Taking on too much and letting others' problems become their own
- Interacting with people who are self-serving and demanding

- Too many unknowns and too much change
- Excessive worrying
- Criticism

What Oranges Need to Function Effectively:

- Respect from their superiors, peers, and subordinates
- Positive feedback and approval
- Friendly, amicable environments
- Structured, secure workplaces with opportunities to help people
- Relationships that are reciprocal in caring and sensitivity
- Tasks that harness their organizational skills

When Dealing with Oranges, Do . . .

- Listen, listen, and listen some more. Don't tune them out.
- Encourage them to share their feelings, concerns, and suggestions.
- Be supportive and verbalize your appreciation.
- Alleviate their worries by explaining what's going on.
- Help them so that they don't feel as if they're carrying the burden of responsibility alone.
- Explain how they can help you, and draw on their organizational and people skills.
- Be sensitive to their need for stability and security.
- Offer support in stressful times.
- Give them advance notice of any changes that will affect their schedule or workload.

- Be respectful of their needs and sensitive to their moods.
- Give them the time they need to make decisions.

When Dealing with Oranges, Don't . . .

- Criticize them for being emotional.
- Try to fix how they're feeling.
- Take them for granted.
- Make commitments you can't keep.
- Give them the silent treatment.
- Be unkind or insensitive.
- Be demanding, domineering, or controlling.
- Put them in confrontational situations.
- Forget to say "Thank you."
- Overload them with the things you don't want to do.
- Force them to make immediate decisions.
- Burden them with your problems.

The Orange World:
*Whenever you set out to do something,
something else must get done first.*

※　※　※

CHAPTER SIX

The Yellow Personality: It's All about Productivity

The information in this chapter is intended to offer a comprehensive overview of the Yellow personality that can be used as a reference guide. It's presented from a pragmatic management perspective whether dealing with superiors, interacting with peers, or managing subordinates. It's intended to be both useful and directly applicable. I've addressed the most relevant aspects of the Yellow's behavioral patterns and neurology—including personality, learning, management, communication, and teamwork styles—and have concluded with a brief overview that can be easily accessed when a situation doesn't warrant a lengthy explanation.

Yellows at a Glance

Yellows are self-confident leaders who are at ease with the responsibility that comes along with high-ranking positions—in fact, they can't keep themselves from directing others. They're ambitious, know what they want, and aren't afraid to take on the challenges necessary to ensure their success, priding themselves on their ability to work smarter and not harder. Their take-charge personas coupled with their ability to motivate and engage people make them effective, charismatic managers. Yellows know how to work a crowd and get people to jump on the bandwagon. They have so much self-confidence that other people seldom question their ability to produce results.

They're keen observers, make decisions easily, and are instinctively political, which helps them find ways to circumvent organizational turf wars and minutiae if either slows down their progress. Yellows are masterful at playing politics if it's necessary for getting ahead and are careful to align themselves with those who can help carry them to the top. They're loyal to their close associates and work comfortably and effectively with them as long as they think that these people are trustworthy.

Yellows' skills lie in their ability to troubleshoot, create strategies, develop systems and procedures, devise action plans, establish policies, and direct others in reaching the goals created through their visionary talents. They're futuristic in their focus and natural problem solvers. They want to do things differently and better and resist sticking with the norm, looking for patterns in everything as a means of gaining understanding and coming up with innovative solutions. They love challenges—the more complex the better. Yellows won't take no for an answer, nor will they follow the path of least resistance. They believe that everything can be accomplished if they just have enough time to think it through. They're mental people who live in their heads and explore the realm of infinite possibilities.

These natural team builders enjoy every aspect associated with growing an organization. They're good at creating concepts, developing structures, and placing people in the right jobs. Yet they aren't heavy-handed, overly controlling, or inclined to resort to "my way or the highway" methodology. Instead, they use the Tom Sawyer approach to get people so interested in participating that they'll automatically want to jump in.

Yellows thrive on creating strategies and then making them work. When something mentally tantalizes them, they'll throw themselves completely into the project until it comes to fruition. They're perfectionists and true workaholics. However, if you ask them why they work so much, they'll tell you it's because their jobs are their playtime.

Ten Predictable Behavioral Traits of a Yellow Personality

Here are ten of the most predictable and observable behavioral traits of Yellows. Each one contributes to their natural problem-solving abilities. Although other personality colors may display similar behaviors, a Yellow will demonstrate them more consistently and frequently.

1. Ambitious. Yellows believe in setting high standards for themselves. They're goal oriented—determined, intense, tenacious, and singularly focused when it comes to seeing that their objectives are met. These achievement-motivated individuals aren't timid about displaying their ambitious natures. They seek to excel in everything, even on their first try. Failure isn't an option for Yellows.

2. Ethical. Yellows have very high standards, which are used as the basis for self-conduct and to measure their involvement with others. They're fair, honest, trustworthy, and truthful. If people question their intentions, they become indignant, verbally aggressive, and openly confrontational. It helps to remember that it's okay to examine their decisions more closely, but never doubt their integrity.

3. Self-confident. Yellows believe in themselves. They're neither timid nor meek, and they don't give in to scare tactics or succumb to their fears. Instead, they'll muster up the courage needed to face whatever challenges come their way and move forward with confidence and determination. They have an inner knowledge that their purpose in life is to make a difference, and it's their self-confidence and persevering nature that makes achieving their dreams possible.

4. Tenacious. *Impossible* isn't a word in Yellows' vocabulary. They can't even relate to it, especially when it comes to finding a better way to do things. When they want something and set their minds to getting it, it's best to stay out of their way because their tenacious nature makes them formidable. They have the ability to make things happen even when other people don't believe they can be done.

5. Visionary. Their futurist focus and their ability to think out of the box makes Yellows masterful visionaries. They're able to anticipate needs and create innovative solutions. The most motivating thing for Yellows to hear is "What if," because those words excite their imaginations and stimulate their thinking. They're always looking forward, trying to forecast what's going to happen—it's like candy for their minds.

6. Skeptical. Yellows tend to be suspicious of everyone and everything. Trusting isn't their first instinct, so they'll usually take a "wait and see" position until they're sure that others' words and actions coincide. Yellows are quick to size people up and rely on their first impressions to decide if these individuals are worth developing a relationship with. If the initial evaluation is favorable, they're more inclined to take the next step; but if it isn't, they'll write these folks off and avoid any kind of interaction.

7. Reserved. Yellows are reserved and use their standoffish, aloof demeanor as a means of keeping others at arm's length. Consequently, it's difficult to be around them and even tougher to get to know them. People see these individuals as unapproachable, complex, and narcissistic. This works just fine for Yellows because it keeps others, even those close to them, from discovering their insecurities and vulnerabilities.

8. Cerebral. The most important part of the body for Yellows is their brain. They're deep thinkers who spend a lot of time "in their heads," and they see their mental acuity as being their most valuable asset. They believe that everyone should continually seek to learn, expand their skills, and create original thoughts. Those who are mentally lazy and won't think for themselves aren't the kind of people Yellows generally choose to be around.

9. Fiercely independent. Yellows need the freedom to do things for themselves. They don't want other people telling them what to do or how to do it. They'll rarely seek other people's opinions or advice because they want to draw their own conclusions and do things their way. They won't allow others to control them, nor are they interested in being in relationships that require being accountable to anyone else—superiors, peers, employees, or mates.

10. Nonconformists. Yellows want to be seen as being different, so they'll resist following what's tried-and-true. Their defiant, independent nature motivates them to write their own rules rather than following societal norms. They can't be intimidated into doing things they don't want to, nor are they willing to forgo their individuality to comply with outside expectations. They regard themselves as icono-clasts and enjoy coloring outside the lines.

Personality Style

YELLOW PERSONALITY

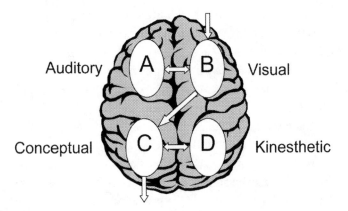

Yellows' personality quadrant combination preference is B and C. They begin gathering information on the right side of the brain, then move to the left side to make decisions. However, their neurology is different from the other three colors because while their favorite combination is working with information, they're also simultaneously using their other quadrants, too. In effect, they're jumping between all quadrants of the brain and drawing upon each to assist them in processing data and decision making. If this sounds confusing, just try being inside Yellows' brains!

114

The upside of this neurology is that they can move freely among all the quadrants to gain different perceptions of the same situation. The downside is that they get so caught up in the jumping around that they tend to suffer from "analysis paralysis," meaning that they get too much information too fast with too many possibilities—and not enough time to think things through thoroughly. Let me say it in another way: Yellows begin gathering input in the right brain by looking for patterns, jump to the left brain to make sense of them, move back to the right to be sure everything truly does match, go back to the left again to make a logical decision, and then return to the right once more to be sure that the process and data feel right emotionally. It's tiring just to think about!

However, it should be noted that even though they briefly touch on the emotional decision-making quadrant, they don't place any value on what it offers and will resort to relying on their logic for the final say. If you've ever been around Yellows, you can attest to the fact that they need time to think things through; and if they're pressed, they may become aggressively defensive. It's their neurological jumping around that explains why they need time to process things.

Despite all this—or perhaps because of it—Yellows' greatest asset is the mind. They're independent thinkers who pride themselves on being able to utilize and integrate their logic, intuition, and imagination to come up with creative solutions. Their inventive nature finds great pleasure in coming up with ways to do things differently and make them better. It doesn't matter to Yellows if it's never been done before or if it didn't work in the past; they're confident that if they can conceive it, they can achieve it. They know very well that if all else fails, they can fall back on their resourcefulness and determination.

They tend to be involved in the cutting edge of technology and in the design and creation of new products. They're intense people and passionate conceptualizers who become singularly focused once they set their minds on something that intrigues them.

Their ability to utilize all quadrants makes them effective at finding answers when others can't. They're masterful in how they troubleshoot to identify issues before they even develop. Consequently, they focus on prevention. It isn't uncommon for Yellows to mentally play out scenarios, contemplating what they'll do in a given situation and holding internal conversations preparing for what they'll say if they're asked a particular question. Their credo is the same as the Boy Scout motto: "Be Prepared."

Yellows want to be identified as being part of the solution and not the problem, so they have very little tolerance for those who dwell on difficulties. It's incomprehensible to them that people won't help themselves and that they'd choose to stick with what they've done in the past rather than try something different. The problem is that Yellows fail to remember that not every personality color is as solution oriented as they are.

The best word to describe Yellows is *self.* They're self-starters, self-assured, self-confident, self-reliant, self-motivated, and self-made. In fact, they don't believe they need other people to achieve results. Nothing irritates them more than when others take it upon themselves to tell them what to do. Should you ever find yourself in this kind of situation, don't be surprised if Yellows become sarcastic, tactless, and emotionally cutting in their strong verbal reactions.

Yellows want the freedom to think for themselves and use their intellectual capabilities to expand their minds through the pursuit of both knowledge and wisdom. Due to their logical nature, they don't need to express their emotions. They're private people who keep things to themselves, which can make it difficult to know where you stand with them. However, this isn't meant to imply that they aren't sensitive, because they are—and in fact, they're prone to getting their feelings hurt. They just believe that it's better to keep their emotions buried inside rather than inviting someone to use the information against them in a conflict situation. The only time Yellows will open up is if they feel that they can trust a person implicitly. When this happens, it's usually with another Yellow.

Those in this color are never content with the status quo or following someone else's lead. They see rules as being for people who aren't willing to make their own. Their independent nature makes them loners. Consequently, others believe that Yellows aren't good team players. This is understandable because of their natural aversion to following and doing things in the same way everybody else does.

Yellows want to produce results their own way and find ingenious solutions to both technical and personal problems. They aren't afraid of the unknown, tackling difficult problems, or doing something for the first time; and they won't under any circumstance follow the path of least resistance. They enjoy the adrenaline rush of a new challenge and aren't hesitant about questioning, pushing, or prodding others in the process, whether they're attacking systems, rules, or authority in general. They'll persevere until they get what they need to achieve their objectives. While this may be seen as a positive quality in a leader, it makes them difficult to control. It's even harder to predict what they're going to do next, which can make others uncomfortable about following Yellow supervisors.

It's important for Yellows to be their own people and feel in control of their own destinies. They're not willing to put their fate in another's hands, even if it's someone they trust. They want to be the captains of their own ships and will aggressively confront anyone who tries to put them in a subordinate role. These self-reliant personalities are perfectly content being alone, and while they understand the need for help in getting ahead, they don't long for company so strongly that they're willing to give up their identity or autonomy.

Yellows are only interested in involving themselves with those they view as equals. They don't intend to become involved in relationships that are emotionally complex or require them to adjust their behavior. This is true both at work and at home. They want to be with people who will compliment them, make them look good, respect them, and be content letting them lead. They look for connections that encourage individuality and offer the freedom they need to pursue their personal and professional interests.

By nature, Yellows are skeptical and suspicious, so they enter into relationships with some trepidation. They want to be sure that people can be trusted before bringing them on board as part of the team. They're keen observers of human behavior and are quick to recognize when someone's words and actions don't match. They aren't interested in entering into any business where those involved don't share their values, ethics, and integrity. Everyone has to prove themselves before Yellows will fully accept them. After accepting them, Yellows expect the new associates to be loyal and steadfast in their support.

Yellows are private people who dislike entrusting others with their feelings. As a result, they avoid lengthy conversations that require displaying sentiment. Their reserved, aloof nature makes it easy for them to remain detached so that they can observe situations. Because Yellows are so different in how they deal with life and its challenges, they tend to create an artificial persona so that no one discovers their idiosyncrasies, insecurities, and vulnerabilities—which they believe could and would be used against them. This facade helps keep people at a distance and serves as a form of self-protection. Consequently, other personalities see them as hard to get to know, standoffish, cold, evasive, and noncommittal . . . which is exactly the way they want it.

Learning Style

The learning style sequence for Yellows is *conceptual, visual, kinesthetic,* and *auditory,* which reveals that they begin the process internally based on the mental pictures and concepts that take shape in their heads. Once ideas are clearly formulated, they move outward to validate things visually, such as through their personal observations or reading. (Yellows are voracious readers.)

If they can support their internal concepts through what they see or read, they'll move forward into the kinesthetic and auditory modes.

As with Oranges, *kinesthetic* refers to Yellows' need to write down their observations and translate what they read into their own words. In the case of the auditory component, Yellows don't rely so much on what they hear as what they say when sharing their concepts and observations. By talking through their thoughts, they're able to better understand them.

Yellows' primary motivation for learning is to gather more information and become expert in whatever subjects and topics interest them. They want to continually expand their consciousness and hone their thinking by using their observation skills to pick up concepts and then devise elaborate theories. The intent is to stimulate thinking and integrate those self-conceived hypotheses into what's known or has been proven.

For people of this color, the process isn't merely about acquiring information; it's about having the time to think things through, contemplate the possibilities, critique the information, determine what's accurate, assign value, and figure out practical applications. Yellows see this as the means of achieving the intellectual competence and personal effectiveness they desire, fulfilling their drive for self-mastery.

They're resourceful and industrious and believe that this exercise is the only way to liberate themselves from the mental barriers potentially blocking their ability to create innovative solutions that will not only address immediate problems, but also potentially eliminate future issues. Yellows see learning as the process of weaving acquired knowledge together with inner wisdom and incorporating both into practical applications. For them, this is an integral part of making progress, dealing with change, stimulating the imagination, and growing both personally and professionally—it's the vehicle to conquer the impossible.

Yellows learn best in traditional settings from instructors whom they consider to be thought-provoking experts in their fields. They're primarily motivated by esteem for those who are teaching them. If Yellows don't respect their instructors' intelligence, then it will be difficult for them to place any value on what's being taught.

They thrive when offered independence and autonomy, while at the same time being challenged to look beyond the obvious. They'll use this environment to forge partnerships, hold theoretical discussions, and share their concepts. The ideal spot for Yellows encourages participation, solicits

questions, promotes thinking out of the box, involves philo-
sophical discussions, and sparks creativity.

Here are some noteworthy qualities of Yellows' learning
style:

Strength:	Creating concepts and solutions, whether unconventional or traditional
Learn by:	Thinking through ideas
Skill:	Tackling problems impersonally, rationally, and logically
Weakness:	Can suffer from analysis paralysis when overwhelmed with too much information too fast
Motivation to learn:	Answer the question "What if?"—"What if we did it this way?" "What if we built a better mousetrap?" "What if that wasn't the real problem?"
Learning objective:	Stimulate thinking and gain new skills
Application:	Present the problem and give them the time to think about it. Follow up with a memo restating the issue and their role in the process, but avoid telling them what to do. Ask for a project timeline, which creates a commitment in

Application (cont'd):   Yellows' minds, forcing them to move into action rather than just continuing to think and analyze.

Management Style

Yellows' management style is characterized by their visionary skills; they're focused on going where no enterprise has gone before. They're looking for innovation not emulation; past performance serves only as a launching platform for future direction. The greatest challenge for Yellow managers is staying in the present to deal with current problems. The excitement of moving a project or an organization into previously uncharted waters makes dealing with mundane repetitive tasks a very low priority. The upside is that the rapidly changing world we live in stimulates and motivates these leaders into achievements matched by no other.

They present their visions complete with fully thought-out goals, benchmarks, and timelines. They anticipate nuances, stumbling blocks, and glitches that may arise in the course of achieving the desired objectives. They assume that this information will be understood and acted upon in the way they want, but this is risky because Yellow minds move at a rate that some other personalities can't match. Consequently, the communication process may break down, to the surprise and dismay of all parties.

Yellow managers will typically take charge with a self-assurance that no one will question. As a result, others will follow their lead freely and support them in any way possible. They're nondirective, meaning that since they don't want anyone telling *them* what to do, they treat their employees accordingly.

While this sounds appealing, unless the staff members are Yellows, they don't understand what's expected of them or how to move forward. This perplexes, disappoints, and even frustrates Yellow managers, because they expect their people to act as independently as they do and use their heads to figure out what needs to be done. The Yellows' perspective is that they did their part—sharing the vision and communicating the action plan—so go take care of business.

Yellows are driven by the need to improve, achieve, and significantly contribute; but in doing so, they can lose touch with reality and their team. When consumed by a problem, project, or situation, interruptions are seen as nuisances, which comes across in their gestures and "Go away—you're bothering me" glares.

This isn't just frustrating. It can create hurt feelings, which lead to interpersonal issues that can't be ignored. Yellows manage tasks, not people, so they tend to surround themselves with Reds and other Yellows because these personality colors are self-directed, problem focused, and solution oriented and don't require any emotional hand-holding. The worst situation Yellows can find themselves in is having to mediate emotional turf wars within their organization. This creates a great deal of resentment in them.

As managers, Yellows tend to make unilateral decisions and are even known to override their own managers or their subordinates if they think it over and believe the wrong choices were made. They're judgmental and opinionated and believe that following their own lead—not anyone else's—will get them where they want to go.

While they're quick to criticize, they're slow to express appreciation. Yellows assume that their staff members know when they're doing a good job, so acknowledging what's obvious isn't only unnecessary, it's also a waste of time. They see it as empty praise and are concerned that people may find it insulting. This isn't to imply that Yellows never commend someone for going beyond the call of duty, because they do. It's just that accolades must be earned.

Yellows are pioneering, cutting-edge, and ingenious leaders who long to make a difference and do things in a fresh way. They inspire others and create a sense of urgency for people to act now and join in their vision. They're analytical, strategic, and forward-thinking, thriving on demanding and complex challenges that require them to draw on their intellectual abilities.

These folks are also competitive, but not like Reds, who pit themselves against others. Yellows compete with themselves, as their personal standards are constantly being challenged. They won't rest on their laurels or take a "wait and see" attitude. They push themselves hard just to see what they're capable of achieving.

This doesn't mean that Yellows won't go after what they want or believe in, because they will. The difference between their competitive nature and that of Reds is that they don't compete to win at the expense of others. Instead, they'll create a situation that's beneficial for everyone, not winning just to prove they can, and not destroying anyone's self-esteem in the process. They aren't mudslinging, backstabbing, or name-calling people, because their inherent politician keeps such behavior in check. Yellows understand the need to not burn bridges; they know that someday down the road they may need the support of their former competitors.

As managers, they aren't interested in being mediocre. They want to be exceptional; stand out from the crowd; and get recognized for their competency, expertise, and ability to get the job done well. Making a good impression is important to them; however, it's not what drives them. They're tough-minded, blunt, and often tactless leaders who cut to the chase in order to get what they need. They can be relentless in their questioning and intolerant of ignorance, excuses, and defeatist behavior as they focus on long-term objectives, which will ensure that today's problems don't become tomorrow's disasters.

These perfectionists demand a lot from themselves and everyone around them. They're enterprising and resourceful and will push the envelope just to prove to themselves that they can. They're confident leaders who look for declining trends, problems, and underlying vulnerabilities in organizations and systems. They'll use all of these as a platform to come up with innovative solutions that will fully utilize their leadership skills.

Communication Style

Yellows perceive themselves as being good communicators and are surprised when other people don't share that perspective. From their point of view, they're articulate, clear, and concise in conveying their thoughts, and careful to think through what they're going to say before they begin speaking.

The real issue is that they spend so much time thinking about what they're going to say and carry on so many internal conversations that they actually think they've said something, when in fact, they haven't. When this happens—which it does regularly—Yellows become critical and accuse others of not listening or paying attention. Talk about a communication problem! Everyone loses in this situation. It's a challenge for both Yellows and the other parties to not lose their cool and become emotionally reactive. In the short term, this creates instant tension, and it could completely break down the lines of communication over time.

Yellows abhor lengthy discussions that rehash the same situation. They don't like to engage in small talk and will avoid conversations that are superficial or emotionally charged. Consequently, they tend to be terse and direct, and—from other colors' perspectives—lacking in social grace. Instead, Yellows prefer to involve themselves in discourse that's mentally stimulating and creates the opportunity for them to share their opinions and knowledge; they like identifying problems, offering solutions, and discussing concepts intended to make people think.

Yellows enjoy a good debate and will belabor a point if they think that others aren't getting what they're trying to convey. They can manipulate words to get what they want and will become verbose and nitpicky when they think that they're right and others are wrong. Their breadth of knowledge and use of language make them engaging conversationalists. However, when it comes to talking about something they don't care for, they become bored and will try to redirect the conversation. If this fails, they'll excuse themselves altogether.

While Yellows think they're good at communicating the essential elements of their vision, they tend to fall short in filling in the blanks or providing necessary direction. As a result, people usually feel left in the dark—unsure of how to proceed. If you find yourself in this situation, ask them for clarity and, most important, tell them what you need from them. This keeps the lines of communication open and prevents failure. Yellows assume that people understand what they're saying, which can quickly create problems that can turn into a power struggle if left unresolved.

Teamwork Style

Being an obedient team member isn't Yellows' strength because of their need for autonomy and independence. They prefer—and usually will orchestrate—being the leader so that they don't have to deal with others telling them what to do or how to do something. When Yellows do become part of a team, it's because they've reconciled in their mind that it's necessary for getting the job done or it's the only way they can move themselves to a superior position. They prefer small groups where decision making doesn't involve a lot of people and each individual can contribute significantly. They believe in lean, mean organizations and find large systems counterproductive, emotionally draining, inefficient, and fraught with problems created by the needs of everyone's egos.

As managers, Yellows contribute their expertise, confidence, and leadership abilities. They're quick to take on challenges, and their presence brings about a sense of stability that others can count on. They're good at developing procedures that will enhance productivity and excel in overseeing the implementation until all the bugs are worked out. Then they're ready to move on to the next project.

Yellows' talents lie in analyzing situations and creating action plans, but they aren't good at staying with something once the challenge is gone and it moves into the maintenance stage where the activities become repetitious. When this occurs, they rely on their staff members to pick up the ball and ensure that things will continue to run smoothly and goals are met. They like:

- Time to reflect and come up with ways to make the team better
- Autonomy and being alone

- The freedom to express their opinions
- Meetings that are focused and conclude with a decisive plan of action
- Being in leadership positions, with the responsibility associated with such
- Taking the role of the group visionary
- Troubleshooting and drawing on their resourcefulness to come up with appropriate solutions

Overview of the Yellow Personality

Basic Needs:
- Mental stimulation and challenges
- Learning opportunities
- Minimal redundancy
- Time to think
- Interaction with people they can trust
- Novelty and change

Strengths:
- Intelligence
- Problem solving
- Self-confidence and self-direction
- Leadership
- Innovation and inventiveness
- Visionary ability
- Competency and expertise
- High standards and integrity

What They Value:

- Loyal relationships
- Theoretical and abstract thinking
- Efficiency and productivity
- Truthfulness
- Decisiveness
- Logic
- Ingenuity

Behavioral Motivations:

- Achievements beyond self-perceived limitations
- Doing things other people can't
- Peer recognition for intelligence
- Control of time
- Desire to make a difference
- Freedom offered by financial security
- Status

Limitations:

- Analysis paralysis
- Impersonal, aloof, and reserved
- Quick to judge
- Understated arrogance
- Excessive need for autonomy
- Capacity to become indifferent in hostile circumstances
- Unwillingness to be subservient
- Unrealistic expectations

Blind Spots:

- Overlook the need to show appreciation or provide feedback
- Assume people listen and understand
- Critical and impatient with those who make excuses
- Terse and insensitive when pushed to make an impulsive decision
- Overwhelmed by too many petty tasks
- Difficulty dealing with redundancy
- Compliance with traditionalism
- Inability to stop solving other people's problems

Insecurities:

- Failure
- Rejection
- Being held accountable for other people's bad decisions
- Being forced to comply with established dictates and practices

Room for Improvement:

- Actively listen without judgment
- Stop pointing out problems
- Communicate patiently and effectively
- Delegate
- Stay present in the moment rather than focusing on the future

Authority Relationships:

- Challenge authority
- Assume parity with higher management

- Prefer minimal management and direction
- Make strategic contributions
- Responsible

Relationships with Peers:
- Stay detached
- Selective
- Supportive only after others have proven themselves trustworthy
- Willing to help those who are interested in drawing on their expertise
- Social; enjoy personal interaction
- Feel camaraderie with other Yellows

Irritations:
- Lack of commitment and follow-through
- Ignorance (perceived or real)
- Dictatorial behavior
- Lack of planning
- Poor time management
- Emotional outbursts
- Being pushed to make a decision with inadequate time to think it through

How They Irritate Other People:
- Apparent arrogance
- Creating trouble by trying to solve everyone's problems
- Making unilateral decisions
- Aloofness
- Nonconformist attitude and behavior
- Limited capacity to play and have fun

- Thinking they have all the answers
- Assumed leadership
- Outspokenness

What Causes Stress:
- Time wasted by others
- Unclear directions
- Overloaded schedules
- Wishy-washy management
- Trying to control the uncontrollable
- Others not following through
- Emotional outbursts
- Ineptitude

What Yellows Need to Function Effectively:
- No defined boundaries
- Structure and organization
- Goals without established processes
- Freedom to think, innovate, and create
- Autonomy and nondirective management
- Capable support
- Appreciation of their achievements
- Discretionary time

When Dealing with Yellows, Do . . .

- Challenge them to use their thinking abilities.
- Appeal to their reasoning, not their emotions.
- Trust their integrity.
- Appeal to their logic.

- Respect their opinions.
- Assign reasonable time parameters.
- Be honest and straightforward.
- Follow through on commitments.
- Be calm, rational, and respectful.
- Be patient with their need to ask questions.
- Include them in the planning process.
- Ask them for their ideas.
- Share control with them.
- Include them in decisions that directly affect them.
- Encourage stimulating conversations.

When Dealing with Yellows, Don't . . .

- Tell them what to do and how to do it.
- Criticize them publicly.
- Interrupt them.
- Ignore their suggestions.
- Talk over them.
- Falsely accuse them.
- Expect them to be followers.
- Ignore or reject them.
- Impose your rules.
- Press them to do something without giving them the time to do it right.
- Expect them to show their emotions.
- Compete unfairly.
- Commit their time without their involvement.
- Try to one-up them.

The Yellow World:
Every problem demands a solution,
and every solution creates new problems.

⚹ ⚹ ⚹

CHAPTER SEVEN

The Green Personality: It's All about the Team

The information in this chapter is intended to offer a comprehensive overview of the Green personality that can be used as a reference guide. It's presented from a pragmatic management perspective whether dealing with superiors, interacting with peers, or managing subordinates. It's intended to be both useful and directly applicable. I've addressed the most relevant aspects of the Green's behavioral patterns and neurology—including personality, learning, management, communication, and teamwork styles—and have concluded with a brief overview that can be easily accessed when a situation doesn't warrant a lengthy explanation.

Greens at a Glance

Greens are driven by needs and desires and wear their hearts on their sleeves. They're emotionally sensitive and get their feelings hurt if they're treated impersonally. These dramatic personalities relate to their outer world via their intuitive hunches. For this reason, they easily and openly share what they're feeling and thinking with anyone who shows interest. They're expressive, never leaving you wondering how they feel about something or someone, are optimistic, and look for the good in everything no matter how bad it appears. Hopeful, compassionate, and passionate, they bring a sense of humor, levity, and excitement to their interactions and activities. They love experiencing new things, taking risks, and seeking adventures that others might avoid. As a result, their lives are full, rich, and usually overscheduled.

Greens are great at embellishing what happens to them and can turn a mundane experience into an exciting escapade and make it so enticing that others will want to try it—even Reds. Life for Greens is never dull, nor is it boring for the people who share it with them. They view the world as if looking through a wide-angle lens. Consequently, there are many opportunities awaiting them, along with an unlimited vision of life's potential.

Redundancy and being controlled are the two things Greens abhor most. They become impatient and confrontational if they feel boxed in, and bored to the point of losing interest if they're required to do the same thing over and over again. They don't excel in managing details, doing paperwork, sitting at a desk without interpersonal contact, or crunching numbers. Their strengths are in their people skills and ability to be creative and rally the troops for a common cause. They have a wonderful capacity to motivate and excite others into responding to causes that they believe in.

Greens have deadline anxiety and will find themselves actually experiencing physical discomfort when pressed to hit someone else's deadlines. Time is vague for them—the opposite of Reds, who view it literally. To Reds, deadlines are cast in concrete. To Greens, they're "soft targets"—that is, they use time so that they have a general idea of when something needs to be done. They divide the day into bite-size pieces so that tasks can be broken down into manageable units not requiring prolonged focus.

These social individuals thrive in environments where interaction is encouraged. They actually restore their energy when dealing with others, while isolation deprives them of the joy of shared experiences and sends them into a tailspin of self-defeating behavior.

Being part of a team is important to them, as is enjoying the camaraderie with those who have similar interests. The word *synergistic* describes a group of Greens working together in a cooperative and cohesive manner. They enjoy brainstorming sessions, as this activity makes it possible for them to create ideas without feeling as though they have to manifest results.

Greens tend to be entrepreneurial and engage in opportunities that are often perceived as high risk by other colors. They can charm, sell, promote, wheel and deal, and have fun at the same time. If they can position themselves with a strong leader and have a supportive team behind them, there's very little a Green can't do.

Ten Predictable Behavioral Traits of the Green Personality

Here are ten of the most predictable and observable traits of Greens. Each one contributes to their ability to be creative, as well as their fun-loving nature. Although other personality colors may display what appears to be similar behavior, Greens will demonstrate these characteristics more consistently and frequently.

1. Expressive. Greens aren't shy about public displays of emotion. Because they make decisions based on emotional judgments, it's important for them to be able to express what, how, and why they're feeling a certain way. This also lets them observe reactions and use that information to determine how to interact. Greens need to tell people how much they're appreciated and how happy they are to have them in their lives.

2. Idealistic. Greens are idealistic and believe in a world that's accepting and unconditional—where everyone is tolerant of each other and there's no conflict or battling. They're so driven by their perception of how things should be that it's a constant struggle for them to deal with mundane activities and not lose touch with reality (a common problem). When these folks say that they need to be more grounded, they're telling the truth.

3. Attention seeking. Greens want to be acknowledged and appreciated and enjoy being the center of attention. If they're extroverted, they'll use their dramatic flair for style and gregarious nature to help them stand out in a crowd. Oblivious to conventions, they create interesting and sometimes eccentric behavior to get others to notice them. They enjoy being different and marching to their own drummer and want recognition for their uniqueness.

4. Enthusiastic. Greens' enthusiasm for life, coupled with their ability to turn the ordinary into the extraordinary, make them enjoyable to be around. They're the Pied Pipers of the personality world. Their primary motivation is encouraging people to feel good about who they are, cheering them on when they're feeling down, and sharing a message of love. Greens inspire excitement, energize, and charm others into wanting to let go of their fears, drop their guard, and open their hearts to whatever experiences life offers. Their enthusiasm is contagious, and their flair is inspiring. They're optimistic, playful, and willing to go with the flow.

5. Active. Both introverted and extroverted Greens seem to have boundless amounts of energy. They're busy people who prefer to keep moving rather than feeling stuck in one place. "A rolling stone gathers no moss" best describes Greens' insatiable need to participate in whatever sounds fun. They believe that life should be enjoyed, rich with activities that involve people they care about.

6. Intuitive. Greens feel vibes and trust their hunches rather than relying on logic or going with what's obvious. Their uncanny ability to read people and know intuitively what's going on makes it difficult to hide anything from them.

7. Creative. Greens love to create for the sheer pleasure of it. They have lots of ideas yet find little need to take any action. They're imaginative, witty, unconventional, enterprising, and continually coming up with new ways to do things. They're bold and adventurous and do best in environments where their abilities are appreciated. Since Greens see the world through the right hemisphere of the brain, they're not bound by the limitations or mental barriers associated with the logical, analytical left side. Consequently, they allow their creativity to flow freely and come up with groundbreaking concepts.

8. Emotionally unpredictable. Greens are moody. When they feel good about themselves, they're fun to be around. But when they're in an emotional funk and aren't happy about their lives, they're pensive, cold, distant, and argumentative. As a result, they'll tend to read negative meanings into everything and will be contrary and stubborn. Because of this, other people see them as fickle and difficult, so they tend to avoid them until they come back to their normal, cheerful Green selves.

9. Changeable. Just when it looks as though Greens are finally settling down and focusing their attention on one thing, they'll throw a curveball by suddenly deciding to do something different. While they usually alter what isn't working, when they get bored it's not unlike them to modify what's going well, too. Change allows them to use their creativity and experience new things. Since they struggle when dealing with redundancy, they'll use variation as a means of adding spice to their lives and for avoiding anything they don't want to do.

10. Adaptable. Greens are spontaneous, flexible, and always open to trying new things. They're attracted to experiences and relationships that allow them to be different and support the unconventional way they see the world. They flourish when they have the freedom to be themselves and follow wherever their hearts lead them. It's easy for them to adjust to whatever's demanded of them and to fit comfortably into any situation. They harness their adaptability in the creative things they do and see it as one of their greatest assets.

Personality Style

GREEN PERSONALITY

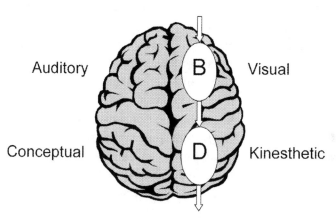

Auditory   B   Visual

Conceptual   D   Kinesthetic

The Green personality quadrant combination prefer-ence is B and D, meaning that they're right-brain domi-nant. Information is gathered through their intuition, which randomly creates images in their mind, and their decision making is based on emotional judgment. Greens rely heavily on hunches and flashes of insight and use their intuition to guide and direct them.

As is the case with Oranges, they're binary in this pro-cess, meaning that decisions are good or bad, right or wrong. They, too, must personalize information in order to relate to it. The combination of these two right-brain quad-rants encourages jumping back and forth so quickly between gathering data and making choices that they appear to make decisions too fast, without really thinking them through—but this isn't the case. Their mental agility allows them to gain clarity more quickly and avoid the limitations created by left-brain thinking. Consequently, their perception of things is more expansive and their decision making more holistic. Their right-hemisphere combination makes it possible for them to find great joy in the creative process and supports their need to march to their own drummer. It also makes it difficult for them to think in the logical, linear manner that's considered the norm.

Greens are idealists who live in a world of rich, vivid imagination—free spirits who like the fact that they're different. They're inspirational and hopeful, and their optimistic nature helps them focus on the positives of life rather than the negatives, allowing them to see only the good in people. When unpleasant things do happen, they'll immediately see them as opportunities to learn and will seek to find the lessons buried in the experiences. Once they find something of value, they'll use it as a catalyst for change—altering their behavior, appearance, friends, jobs, and even intimate relationships.

Greens love change and actually seek it. They don't see it as being a negative, but rather as an exciting element of personal growth and the motivation to fix what isn't working in their lives. While they perceive shifts as positive, this can be very disruptive to others, especially their bosses, because it creates a certain amount of turmoil and chaos and keeps their interactions in a constant state of flux.

When I asked some supervisors about this color's need to change, they unanimously agreed that mixing things up isn't the issue. The trouble is that Greens don't know how to moderate the process, meaning that they don't just alter one thing at a time and then wait for the dust to settle; rather, they switch everything all at once. This is very unsettling to an organization and everyone involved in it.

Because of Greens' propensity for sudden bouts of change, others tend to see them as loose cannons—flighty, fickle, and indecisive. This is certainly not how these folks view themselves. From their perspective, something new is better than sticking with what's familiar, especially if it isn't working anymore.

These are the cheerleaders of the personality world, and their can-do attitude makes them natural motivators. "Live your dream" is their mantra, and they'll use this idea to inspire and encourage others. Yet, while Greens are quick to help other people discover their hidden strengths and talents, they tend to have difficulty finding their own. They struggle with the challenges of life and are always looking for ways to improve themselves. They're perennial students and are drawn to books, workshops, and classes that will help them cope with life, teach them how to create more meaningful relationships, offer ways to express themselves more effectively, and encourage developing their spiritual nature.

Greens must have meaning and purpose. They seek to understand the intricacies of life and discover what they're meant to do. Their quest will often take them off the beaten path, so it isn't unusual for them to become involved in esoteric studies; practice the customs of other cultures; or become involved in mysticism, occultism, and metaphysics. The New Age movement provides a safe haven for Greens to find themselves, express their uniqueness, and explore nontraditional ways of experiencing life. At the same time, it puts them with like-minded people who share similar values and are on the same journey.

Greens possess the gift of highly developed intuition and are able to sense the vibes of what's going on. This extrasensory aspect of their personality gives them the exceptional ability to read between the lines and know instinctively how people are feeling; they're keen observers of words and actions. It helps them gain clarity so that they can uncover hidden agendas and distance themselves from the potential for conflict. They also use this talent to foresee the future and forecast trends. Their uncanny ability to know what's going on with others, coupled with their unusual insight, makes them interesting conversationalists and intriguing people to be around. It also means that they're valuable assets to any organization that relies on innovation and its ability to stay one step ahead of competition in bringing new products to the marketplace.

There are two speeds at which Greens live their lives: full speed ahead or completely shut down. When they're charging forward, it isn't unusual for them to have multiple sentences going at one time, not completing one statement before moving on to the next. They also may not finish what they've started, as they're trying to spin many plates all at once. This compounds their difficulty with focusing—unless, of course, they're doing something they want to do. In that case, this mode is stimulating and exhilarating. Even intro-verted Greens, whose tendency is to conserve their energy, find themselves occasionally falling victim to their inherent desire to do, have, and experience it all.

On the other hand, when they're shut down, you almost need to scrape them off the floor with a putty knife. There's no motivating them to do anything. They're so out of gas energetically and physically that they want to be left alone or just go to sleep.

Creative is the word that best describes Greens. They thrive as artists, poets, writers, actors, and musicians. They're constantly looking for new and different ways to express their creativity and individuality, whether it's through their work, play, hobbies, or relationships. They have many gifts, and their greatest challenge is to learn to direct their attention to one talent at a time to perfect it. Seeing things through to completion isn't one of their strengths. The cliché "jack-of-all-trades and master of none" certainly fits their tendency to not stay with anything long enough to truly excel at it.

Their restlessness also leads them to believe that the grass is always greener on the other side of the fence. As a result, they constantly want to be somewhere else, regardless of where they are. Boredom is a continual problem, so they try hard to avoid redundancy in everything from performing the same tasks, experiencing the same events, or staying in the same relationship too long. They need the stimulation that comes from doing something new.

Greens' self-esteem lives and dies by their emotions. When things are going well, they feel *really* good about themselves; and when life isn't so great, they feel *really* bad about themselves. They need to share this and become hurt when others aren't interested in listening to them or when they're dismissed as being overly emotional.

Those in this color become very uneasy with conflict and will avoid situations that have that potential. They just want everyone to be happy. Unlike Oranges, however, Greens won't suppress their emotions if it's important for them to get something off their chest; and when they do express themselves, there won't be any doubt in your mind that you've obviously hit their hot button.

How can you tell whether you've pushed Greens too far? Their voices will go up several octaves, and then lovely four-letter words will roll off their tongues—and I don't mean the word *love*. When their feelings are hurt or they become angry, these kind, gentle, easygoing personalities become aggressive and confrontational; and their language gets salty.

Greens are chameleons, with the ability to be so flexible and adaptable that they look and act like different colors.

And while this quality is certainly admirable, it can make them appear unpredictable, flighty, and fickle, making others apprehensive about having to interact with them. One minute they can be agreeable, open, and receptive; and the next minute aggressive, controlling, and venomous. When Greens are being true to their color, they're approachable, easy to be around, and joyful and bring a sense of lightheartedness to their interactions. However, when they change their color and go into their Red mode, they're rigid, dogmatic, unreasonable, and closed-minded to anything that smacks of change. When they turn Orange, they become even more emotional and moody and brood, pout, act like martyrs, and get self-righteous. And in their Yellow guise, they can focus, harness their logic, manifest, and move forward effortlessly. They turn being a chameleon into an art form.

Greens actually need even more independence than Yellows do. They crave the freedom to express themselves, pursue their interests, march to their own drummer, and have the ability to do what they want whenever they want. Their perspective is that no one—not their boss, co-workers, or friends—has the right to take away their individuality or demand that they comply with anything they don't believe in. This doesn't mean, however, that they won't look like they're following the rules; they're good at that. But if you really watch them, you'll see that they aren't. Greens pursue happiness, for that's what they value the most. They want to be joyful at work, at home, and in all their relationships.

Learning Style

The learning style sequence for Greens is *visual, kinesthetic, auditory,* and *conceptual,* which reveals that they begin the process based on personal observations, what they literally see, and what they read. Once they get a clear picture of what they need, they move into their kinesthetic mode by putting the information into something they can relate to, meaning that they write it down—literally touching what they're observing or creating a picture of it through doodling and using arrows or lines to connect the pieces and find the patterns. This allows them to internalize the data and relate to it personally. In doing so, they're able to connect with it emotionally to determine whether it's something they're interested in learning. If it is, they'll use this same kinesthetic method to find the words (auditory) needed to express how they're feeling and what they're seeing.

Auditory also refers to their need to talk about their observations and ask others to share their feelings and opinions. Then, based on the verbal feedback they get, Greens will move into the conceptual mode to gain understanding and be sure that their internal picture matches what they really saw.

Because of Greens' tendency to personalize things, the feedback they receive helps them ensure that what they create in their minds is real and not imagined. However, asking for people's perceptions can be tricky, because not all personality colors get the same impression. This is risky, because the feedback Greens get from others ultimately determines not only how they feel about themselves, but how they see themselves as learners. They're the only color that has this quality. If what they hear is positive, they're eager, enthusiastic, and engaged students; if it's negative, they're rebellious, resistant, and disengaged.

Greens are hands-on and learn best through personal experience. They see acquiring knowledge as a self-discovery process, an opportunity for personal growth, and a chance to interact with people. They need the experience to inspire them, feed their imagination, and allow them to share their intuitive insights. They want to find out how to succeed in their personal relationships and manifest their dreams.

Greens believe they can do anything, and this is true, as long as what they're studying interests them. If it isn't exciting, they become bored and restless, and their attention wanders off to more creative things. Most of what fascinates them centers around people—how to connect with them, help them, interact with them better, and deal with differences.

Greens just want everyone to have fun, so they see the learning environment as being more of a social event than academic or professional. They enjoy uncovering mysteries, looking for the hidden meanings behind their experiences, reading between the lines, seeing things that other people can't, and sharing their unorthodox perceptions. They're adventurous in their quest for new information and passionate about their interests. These imaginative folks excel in nontraditional environments.

Greens learn best when allowed to use their intuitive insights to come up with unique and sometimes off-the-wall solutions. An ideal situation encourages creative expression, involves brainstorming, values the sharing of emotions, and isn't so structured that there isn't any time for playful, interactive experiences. They gain wisdom from listening to stories and music, talking to people, reading books, and just jumping in and trying things. Most important, Greens need surroundings that are free of stress and conflict, support and stimulate individual growth, and embrace individuality.

Here are some noteworthy qualities of Greens' learning style:

Strength: Vivid imagination and creativity

Learn by: Hands-on and experiential
                       activities

Skill: Encourage people to act on their
                       own visions

Weakness: Lack of follow-through

Motivation to learn: Answer the question "How?"—
                       "How can we make this more
                       fun?" "How can we make this
                       work?" "How do people feel
                       about this?"

Learning objective: Create new ideas

Application: Involve them in the co-creation
                       process, since they love to dream
                       up ideas and speculate on pos-
                       sibilities. Just give them the overall
                       concept, but don't bury them in
                       details. Listen when they come up
                       with something unique, and when
                       they're through sharing, give them
                       honest, constructive feedback. If
                       you begin your critique before
                       they finish, they'll shut down and
                       avoid further participation.

Management Style

Greens' management style is anything but traditional. They're nondirective managers who abide by the philosophy of no restrictive rules, no living in the past, and no consuming obsession with previous performance. Everything has to do with today and looking forward to the future. Enthusiasm and a zest for life make the workaday world an exciting place to be when under Greens' management.

Their strength is in their ability to excite and motivate others to achieve exceptional results. The rewards are great, the recognition is enthusiastic, and the fun is pervasive. Time on the job is eagerly anticipated rather than dreaded. They give credit for effort and will support, assist, and even get involved personally if that's what it takes to help someone succeed. They reward their team with the joy of life.

If having fun and making money are what life is all about, then the Green-managed workplace is where some people prefer to be. But for those who need structure, well-defined responsibilities, written guidelines for every task assigned to them, and closely monitored supervision, this environment may be greatly unsettling. It requires that each person be comfortable with making their own decisions, for that's how it will be.

Greens want their people to work independently, be self-sufficient, handle their own issues, and come to them only to give updates on the status of tasks and projects. They don't want to be told about problems, nor do they want people to pass the buck. They want to hear the good things that are happening and how their staff members are feeling. In fact, Green managers will rarely even ask their subordinates what's going on because of their own need to not be held accountable. Greens assume that everyone really is doing what they say they're doing and will follow through.

These diplomats are careful not to step on anyone's toes. Their focus is on people, not tasks, and their interests lie in helping others succeed. They're participatory managers who will roll up their shirtsleeves if needed. They supervise in a very personal way, and their employees become their friends.

Greens enjoy social interaction where others can just be themselves and have fun. They always strive for cooperation and have no time for turf wars or insensitivity. They use humor and their heightened sensitivity to diffuse conflict when it arises.

They're staunch advocates for their team and will challenge any rule or change in policy that doesn't put their needs first. Greens truly believe that people are the most important asset to any organization and that the primary directive shouldn't be the bottom line, but what's best for their staff members.

It's important to people in this color to develop good interpersonal relationships where everyone feels that they're truly an integral part of the company and not just showing up for the job. Consequently, they create a climate that promotes personal growth, respects individuality, fosters harmonious interaction, and provides a sense of belonging.

Greens lead by inspiration—coaching, applauding, and providing continual positive feedback. Their friendly, cordial, approachable nature makes them easy to be around and support, and their leadership style consists more of subtle persuasion instead of being heavy-handed. Greens believe it's better to have people engage on their own rather than telling them that they have to help. They're passionate people who believe strongly in their causes.

While preferring harmony, Greens aren't afraid to stand up for their convictions or challenge anyone who tries to discredit them or take advantage of their good nature. They tend to position themselves as representatives of the masses and spokespeople for the need for change and reform. They see their efforts as being aligned with the needs of others and their role as being a liaison between workers and the organization. They effortlessly rally groups together by building rapport with them and showing that they truly care. They're purposeful leaders who, while not political in nature, understand the accoutrements of being a politician—shaking hands, patting people on the back, and singing others' praises—and the need to unite people for a common cause.

Greens receive a tremendous amount of satisfaction from sharing their ideas. They're able to communicate them masterfully so that others will embrace them and be willing to support them by offering the time, energy, and resources needed to bring them to fruition. These folks are skilled at creating networks that will pass on their concepts. Their propensity for taking novel and unorthodox positions makes them attractive to like-minded individuals. However, from Reds' perspective, Green leaders are irresponsible and unrealistic because of their lack of respect for tradition and their inability to create clear, concise, and concrete action plans.

Communication Style

Greens believe that the quality of their interactions is directly tied to their ability to communicate effectively—in other words, when they're able to openly and freely share their emotions, they feel good about the relationship. However, when the lines break down, so does the Greens' desire to interact with the person.

Communicating with this color can be tricky, since it's frequently difficult to know where they are, emotionally or mentally. When their feelings are hurt, they're good at giving off the illusion that everything's fine, even though it really isn't. It's easy to trigger an outburst without understanding why.

Inwardly, Greens' minds are continually jumping around from one thought to another and can become so preoccupied that they literally don't hear most of what's being said. If this is the case, it's difficult to get on the same wavelength with them and get their attention focused on the conversation.

To effectively communicate with these folks, you have to develop the ability to read nonverbal signals such as their body language and eye contact. You can't rely just on what they say or what you hear. Watch for the telltale warning signs alerting you that there's unhappiness brewing or that something you said stepped on their toes. It also helps to remember that while you're reading their body language, they're reading yours. This may explain why you sometimes find yourself dealing with an unexplained communication breakdown. It isn't because of what you said; it's because of how they read the nonverbal clues you gave when you said it.

While there are many unpredictable aspects to Greens' behavior, when it comes to the communication process, they're extremely predictable. They personalize everything and will make all conversations focus on them. When they're happy and feel good about themselves, the discussions are upbeat, positive, focused on the future, and animated and involve both talking and listening. Next, they'll always speak from the heart and expect others to do the same. When they don't feel as if people are being honest, they'll become silent and withdraw from the conversation. In situations such as this, Greens become distressed, disappointed, and angry and even feel an element of betrayal. Last, if they're unhappy or feeling put-upon, then talks will mostly involve listening to them getting their emotions off their chest.

If they're feeling mistreated or underappreciated, they'll become cold and silent and avoid any interaction at all. The best thing to do when this happens is to bring the problem to the surface immediately. Don't try to ignore it, dismiss it, or sweep it under the rug, hoping that it will go away; and don't just chalk it up to their having another emotional meltdown. Most important, even if you might be thinking it, never, ever utter the words "There you go being emotional again." A comment like this could land you in the doghouse for hours, days, or even weeks. Greens are very good at using the silent treatment to get the point across when you've said or done something that hurt their feelings.

The best way to handle a crisis like this is to encourage them to talk and share how they're feeling, and ask them to explain what you did wrong so that you can avoid repeating it in the future. This approach will immediately defuse the situation and open up the lines of communication once again.

Here are a few other mistakes that can be made when communicating with a Green:

- Treating them impersonally
- Using a condescending tone of voice
- Talking down to them
- Making patronizing comments
- Talking about them as if they weren't there

All of these situations will upset them and set off a barrage of unpleasant reactions, ranging from a mere expression of their displeasure to shouting to being verbally vicious.

It's best to remember that when it comes to communicating, Greens are binary—they're either responsive or reactive, and the former is much more pleasant to deal with.

Teamwork Style

Greens enjoy every aspect of being a part of a team: camaraderie, social interaction, helping out, encouraging one another, and sharing common goals and interests. They're supportive and bring an element of lightness to the group. They're able to see the potential in people and appreciate individual contributions. They understand that working with others allows them to do what they're good at, while at the same time making it possible for them to delegate things that are difficult for them.

Teams provide the emotional connection Greens need, including the opportunity to laugh, share stories, and bond with their co-workers—something they value highly. They enjoy the competitiveness and bantering that comes with working with people they like, and who share similar interests. These are the folks who energize and motivate others with their enthusiasm and humor. They're skilled at gaining a consensus by sharing their insights and creating a fun cooperative environment.

They strive to make everyone feel as if they belong, and openly acknowledge that their presence and input are an integral part of the group's success. They want others to feel comfortable sharing their emotions, so they'll actively solicit input by asking people how they feel about something and how they'd like to see things happen. They use a democratic approach in dealing with problems or setting goals.

As team members, Greens see it as their role to be mentors, counselors, coaches, and cheerleaders. They like:

- Harmonious and cooperative work environments
- The freedom to create
- Social activities, both at work and on their own time
- Friendships
- Focusing on others
- Positive feedback
- Approval and acceptance

Overview of the Green Personality

Basic Needs:
- Close personal relationships
- Minimal time deadlines
- Flexibility and spontaneity
- Individuality
- Personal recognition
- Change
- Downtime to do what they want
- Social interaction
- New experiences
- Creative expression

Strengths:
- Supportive and attentive
- Creative
- Adaptable
- Sensitive

- Lighthearted
- Optimistic
- Open-minded
- Even disposition
- Motivators
- Instigators

What They Value:
- Happiness
- Love
- Sensitivity
- Emotional expression
- New experiences
- Time to play
- Being addressed by name
- Direct management

Behavioral Motivations:
- Acceptance
- Socially based incentives
- Group involvement
- Helping others

Limitations:
- Lack of sustained focus
- Poor time management
- Not detail oriented
- Excessive personalization
- Constant need for change
- Nonconformists
- Not willing to stick with what's tried-and-true

- Flighty and fickle
- Ungrounded

Blind Spots:
- Too trusting and naïve
- Focus more on people's needs than tasks at hand
- Tend to look to the future and ignore the present
- Hold themselves responsible for anything that goes wrong
- Drive themselves at a burnout pace
- Assume people will do what they say
- Make projections and assumptions without adequate facts and support
- Unable to cope with conflict
- Tend to idealize rather than face reality

Insecurities:
- Being controlled
- Being alone
- Doing something wrong
- Not being accepted

Room for Improvement:
- Assertiveness
- Time management
- Deadline sensitivity
- Becoming less self-absorbed
- Managing emotional volatility
- Organizational skills
- Unpredictability
- Allowing enough time for personal activities

Authority Relationships:

- Responsive to directives
- Uncomfortable with micromanagement
- Idealistic expectations of supervisors
- Require heightened sensitivity to their feelings
- Need direct communication and personal interaction with superiors

Relationships with Peers:

- Cheerful and friendly
- Fickle and critical
- Competitive
- Focused on team needs and goals rather than their own
- Proactive in initiating change
- Build mutually satisfying friendships
- Enjoy sharing social time

Irritations:

- Being treated impersonally
- Deadlines
- Being controlled
- Being told what to do and when to do it
- People not listening
- Hostile environments
- Untrustworthiness

How They Irritate Others:

- Fickleness
- Not following through on their commitments
- Jumping to conclusions

- Being judgmental
- Placing too much value on effort and not enough on producing results
- Inability to stay focused on the task at hand
- Insensitive to time deadlines
- Talking over people

What Causes Stress:
- Emotional overload
- Conflict
- Time pressures
- Unfriendliness
- Inadequate financial security
- Dealing with difficult people

What Greens Need to Function Effectively:
- Conflict-free environment
- Positive feedback and praise
- Stable working conditions
- Personal recognition
- Opportunity for creative expression
- Tasks that harness their people skills

When Dealing with Greens, Do . . .

- Show interest in their ideas.
- Appreciate their creative abilities.
- Let them express themselves without interruption or criticism.
- Use their names when speaking to them.

- Involve them in the co-creation processes.
- Be sincere in your praise, compliments, and appreciation.
- Be sensitive to their need for individuality.
- Support their desire for artistic expression.
- Show interest in them and their pastimes.
- Involve them in planning social activities.
- Accept their spontaneous nature.
- Give clear instructions in writing, since they're visual.
- Provide incentives that are based in social activities.
- Be sincere and engaged when communicating.
- Encourage them to share their feelings.
- Pass them the tissues and let them cry if they get weepy.

When Dealing with Greens, Don't . . .

- Overload them with details instead of just giving them the concept.
- Criticize them for being emotional.
- Try to fix how they're feeling.
- Control or micromanage their activities.
- Talk down to them or be condescending.
- Assume that it's a bad thing if they cry.
- Expect them to embrace redundancy.
- Think that they'll follow rules and policies.
- Pin them down or back them into corners.
- Use strong expressions of anger.
- Be insensitive to their caring nature.

- Ignore them or take them for granted.
- Criticize their need to be social.
- Nag them about finishing a project.
- Immediately say no without hearing every bit of what they have to say.

The Green World:
No amount of genius can overcome an obsession with detail.

❋ ❋ ❋

PART III

APPLYING THE UNDERSTANDING OF PERSONALITY

"It's a four-color workplace. When each color functions from their strength, productivity increases, results are achieved, and the interaction between people becomes less stressful."

— Carol Ritberger

CHAPTER EIGHT

It Takes All Four Colors to Make the Workplace Hum

Imagine living in a monochromatic world: No blue sky, green grass, red fire engines, or orange pumpkins. It would be just a dull black-and-white existence, with nothing to stir our imaginations or make our juices flow. Our world would be understimulating and boring, to say the least. Ditto if we lived with just a single personality color, so let's take a walk down One-Color Lane—no, let's take four walks, one down Each-Color Lane. To use a favorite Yellow expression: "This will be interesting!"

The World According to Red

We'll start with a 100 percent Red world. First off, we find ourselves living in the world of today based on the lessons of yesterday. Nothing new and innovative clutters our daily activities. If it worked in the past, it works in the present and will continue to do so in the future. The status quo is our template; and our affinity is for rules, procedures, and laws. We have no need to defend them against innovators because all invention is now a derivative or evolutionary outgrowth of something that has previously served us well. If it's not broken, we aren't going to waste our time fixing it.

We follow the dictates of the organization chart to the letter. Lowly Number Fives can talk only to Number Fours, who report to Number Threes, and so on up the line. Number Ones concern themselves with the mission of the company and are oblivious to the daily activities of Number Threes on down. They (the Fives, Fours, and Threes of the world) are there to produce results, not to personalize their situation, and certainly not to create emotional turmoil. In fact, feelings are limited to outbursts of anger over territorial encroachment or celebrations of achievement in besting some rival in the throes of a competitive situation.

Social encounters may focus on comparative evaluations of personal success in terms of possessions, the accomplishments or attractiveness of partners or offspring, or planned travels and adventures. There may also be energetic and vociferous pronouncements of political, religious, or athletic-team preferences, which are defended with energy and unwavering conviction . . . and loud voices.

A solely Red world would be filled with stoic achievement and the continuation of historically based progress. It would be lacking in excitement and emotional responses to all stimuli emanating from off-the-wall thinking. It would personify stability and predictability.

The World According to Orange

Let's journey down the Orange path. A world of this color would be one of constant, passive-aggressive compassion. Decisions would consider the human side of every issue before the business side, looking first at how the world would handle each element of change and the accompanying stress it might generate. Human suffering and indignities perpetrated on society would be minimal. The focus would be on families—personal, local, national, and global communities.

An all-Orange world would decry violence while holding everyone responsible for their personal acts. Punishment for bad deeds would be first in the form of rehabilitation rather than recrimination. The good in each individual would be honored, respected, and enabled. Society would focus on creating a world wherein all of humankind could live in peace and harmony.

Truly, if everyone accepted each other's differences, there would be no contentious issues. Wars would no longer serve a purpose because there'd be nothing to fight over. Saints and deities of all faiths would share equally in global houses of worship. Political aggression would disappear from the face of the earth because each nation would share its bounty freely. The haves would tend to the have-nots, asking for no more in return than a simple thank-you.

The Orange organization would function under the old-school concept of getting out there and talking to the troops. Each manager, regardless of placement on the organization chart, would spend time listening to opinions and suggestions from everyone working there, whatever their position or income level. The company would function as a family with all the employees feeling as if they were a part of the whole process, and they'd all be valued for their individual contributions.

Involuntary release from a job would be preceded by multiple attempts to retrain, remotivate, or rehabilitate. Only when all attempts to retain the employee had failed would the release take place, and then outplacement assistance would be offered.

An Orange world would be one of caring and compassion, with a focus on supporting and encouraging success and nurturing everyone on an equal basis. It would truly be a world of boundless humanity.

The World According to Yellow

Now we're going to venture down the Yellow brick road to the world of zero problem tolerance. From this perspective, we should participate fully in life and perpetually remain on the cutting edge. Yellows don't advocate problem solving, but prefer prevention. It's much more logical to foresee and forestall than to solve and repair. In this world, the focus is on enhancing the quality of life for everyone through the utilization of all the tools that intelligent, creative minds can conceive.

Consider the Yellow world as being a giant think tank where every issue and problem could be addressed and dealt with from a logical, well-thought-out approach. Greed, corruption, violence, and crime aren't logical in this world, therefore they don't exist. In their place are the minds of leadership focusing their attention on the needs of society and meeting them sufficiently to eliminate societal ills. Issues such as illiteracy, poverty, plagues, and famine are all solvable, given the focused energies of Yellows. Utopia can't exist except by harnessing the powers of the mind in order to understand how to define it, design it, and overcome the obstacles that stand in the way.

In the Yellow organization, minds work so that hands may create. Productivity issues are under constant and regular assessment to minimize wasted time, energy, and resources. Everyone, from the bottom of the organization to the top, is recognized and rewarded for enhancing output. Efficient use of time and materials encourages profit sharing and success. It's a world of conserving resources through continually exploiting the advances of technology.

A Yellow world would focus not on the past and how things have always been done, but on the future and how things might be done better.

The World According to Green

Now we're in Green-land, the last of our visits to a one-color world—and what a place it is. Excitement and laughter run rampant. Every gathering is at once exhilarating, exhausting, and stimulating; every meeting is a party and every party is a meeting. Everything is happening all at once, with no time to breathe. The wonderful world of Green is meant to be enjoyed, loved, and cherished.

Flexibility and compliance are the hallmarks of Green society. If it feels good, do it; if it feels bad, change it; and if it lacks feeling, run away from it. The objective is to plan ahead and stick with the plan—but only if and when the time is right. Change is the rule of the day . . . or is it the week? Life is meant to be a joyful adventure, not filled with a series of grungy tasks. Make everything fun; and anger, unpleasantness, and disagreement cease to exist.

Our Green world carries with it an unrelenting burden of personal responsibility. Each person feels the weight of every failure and shortcoming, both personal and societal. This guilt permeates all thinking and drives global behavioral patterns.

The Green organization is a continual work in progress and exists in a constant state of flux. What functions well today may or may not do so tomorrow because the rules might change. And these shifts are the stimulant that ignites the motivation to participate. Without variation, dullness takes over and redundancy lulls even the most driven employees into distraction. Instead, this place is exhilarating, captivating, exciting, and just plain fun. Creativity and showmanship are universally practiced, but facilitating is a challenge. It's much easier and more enjoyable to come up with a wonderfully inventive solution to a problem than it is to deal with the mundane tasks of bringing it to fruition.

A Green world would be one of joy, laughter, and fun where tomorrow never comes and today is a hoot.

A Functional Four-Color Workplace

Now let's take a look at a fictitious business, the Utopian Widget Works, where every task is assigned to the person most qualified to do it based on their personality color. For this scenario, we won't address how everyone got to be where they are in the company, just how they mesh together to meet its needs.

The Utopian Widget Works was founded many, many years ago by Hubert Utopia, the father of Rupert Utopia the First (Yellow), a brilliant tinkerer and inventor of the Original Digital Midget Widget. All prior attempts to midgetize widgets had met with unqualified failure. They were either unreliable in their mechanisms and failed to operate as intended, or they were too large and cumbersome to qualify as having been midgetized at all. (In effect, they were standard widgets packaged in very tight boxes to disguise their actual bulk.)

Rupert Utopia the First assumed the management of the family business when his father retired. On that fateful day, R. U. the 1, as he was affectionately called, asked the two senior managers to tell him about their departments and the people who worked for them. He intended to introduce the Original Digital Midget Widget as a new product and was concerned about whether it could be produced by the existing employees.

First, he talked to the product manager (Red) who was responsible for design, procurement, and production. His chief designer held a master's degree in design, and had graduated first in her class at a prominent design school in California. She (Green) was ably supported by two junior designers (Green and Yellow), a draftsman (Red), and an administrative assistant (Orange).

His procurement department was staffed by two very knowledgeable people (Oranges) who spent all their time developing relationships with component sources so that they could provide the parts necessary for the manufacture of the company's products. And the production department consisted of an assembly line capably run by ten product assemblers (Reds and Oranges) who had worked together comfortably for more than nine years.

Satisfied with that side of the business, R. U. the 1 then talked to the customer-service manager (Orange). He was responsible for marketing, sales, shipping, receiving, and accounting, including billing, accounts receivable, payroll, and bookkeeping.

His marketing manager (Green) had an extensive background in advertising with a prominent agency prior to joining UWW. Her staff of graphic designers (Greens and Reds) and copywriters (Greens and Yellows) produced award-winning print ads every year.

The sales manager (Red) pressed the salespeople (Greens and Reds) to exceed their goals every month with incentives, good commission plans, and annual recognition events.

Support functions and order taking (Oranges), shipping and receiving (Reds and Oranges), and all accounting functions (Oranges) were staffed by long-term experienced employees.

By the time R. U. the 1 finished his capability review, he was ecstatic. Never in his past business experience had he been part of a company that enabled everyone on the payroll to work in the job they were best suited for. *Look out, world!* he thought. *Here comes the Original Digital Midget Widget.*

It Takes All Four Colors

Make your choice: Could you truly exist in a one-color society? Could society work in a one-color world? Probably not for long. The paradox of our human existence is that we all treasure personal independence and count on personal interdependence. Management's challenge is to understand the distinctively individual motivations and contributions of each personality color and blend them into a tapestry of productive achievement.

The information in the following chapters will help you accomplish this as it delves deeper into the dynamics of personality and offers suggestions on how you can use the understanding of personality to create the results you desire. When those goals are met, you have effective management.

▨ ▨ ▨

CHAPTER NINE

Communication and Conflict

We all want to be heard and responded to—and even more important, understood. The objective of communication is to see that each of these expectations is met by creating an equal exchange of both talking and listening. Here are some general overall hints that will increase the effectiveness of this process:

1. Verbal communication requires being mentally engaged in the process, meaning that you must pay attention to what's being said. Don't just think about what you're going to say next.

2. If you can learn to *actively listen* to the words a person uses, you'll discover that they're disclosing their personality neurology. Then all you have to do is incorporate their preferred words when talking to them. This simple hint can significantly reduce the potential for frustration and minimize the conflict that occurs when what's being said is heard in another way.

3. If people use the word *think* repetitively in their conversations—perhaps by saying, "This is what I think," or "Here are my thoughts"—there's a good chance that they're

Reds or Yellows, because their personality neurology requires that they make decisions based on logic. These folks are providing information in a direct, impersonal manner, which is true to their colors.

If people use the word *feel* over and over—perhaps by saying, "This is how I feel," or "My feelings are"—there's a good chance that they're Oranges or Greens, because their personality neurology requires that they make decisions based on emotions and what feels right. Oranges and Greens are expressing what's in their heart about the information they're sharing, which is true to their colors.

4. Nonverbal communication requires that you participate emotionally in the process, meaning being sensitive to how things are said and paying attention to facial expressions, eye contact, and physical gestures.

5. Watch people's body language because it will tell you their personality neurology and if they're being compromised in the communication process. If they touch their head repeatedly in a conversation, it reveals that they're thinking about what's being said. These gestures can include rubbing their head, wiping their eyes, cleaning their glasses, running their fingers through their hair, rubbing their face or chin, and basically any repetitive movement above the shoulders. This tells you that there's a good chance that they're Reds or Yellows and their personality neurology places a greater importance on what they're thinking than what they're feeling in their heart.

6. If people touch their chest by putting one or both hands on it while talking, rub their shoulders, pat their chest, or cross their arms over their body, there's a good chance

they're Oranges or Greens and their personality neurology places a greater importance on how they feel than the thoughts going through their head. Their body language reveals that they're making a heartfelt emotional decision. They're conveying how they feel, not about the words that are being spoken, but about you.

How to Communicate with Reds	
DO:	*DON'T:*
Be clear about what you want to say before you begin.	Use words that are emotionally charged or that will elicit an emotional reaction.
State the facts and stick to the point.	Ask *why* questions, or they'll give you an emotional response that probably won't be what you're expecting.
Keep your thoughts concise.	Ask them how they feel about something.
Tell them what you're trying to get across and then show them through visual aids. They're auditory first and need you to give them the picture verbally.	Change the subject mid-sentence or leave sentences incomplete.
Draw upon past experiences they're familiar with to make your point.	Repeat yourself. (It's okay for them to, but not you.)
Ask them *what* they think so that they'll respond logically.	Waste their time exploring ideas or discussing concepts. Instead, come to them when you have something tangible.

| How to Communicate with Reds (cont'd) ||
DO:	DON'T:
Always be prepared to support what you're saying.	Skirt around issues rather than telling it like it is.
Minimize small talk.	Put them in a position where they have to defend what they're saying, because they'll take an aggressive posture.
Be assertive and self-confident.	
Avoid emotional outbursts.	
Stress how the information will benefit them.	
Tell them how they can put the data to immediate use.	
Focus on what you want them to hear.	
Expect frankness and bluntness.	
Cut to the chase; don't provide opinions.	
Appeal to their desire to do what's right.	
Understand their need to be in control.	
Use the KISS method of communication—Keep It Simple Statements that will allow them to listen and hear.	

Phrases That Get Reds' Attention

- I have the documentation to support what I'm saying.
- This will save you time and increase your productivity.
- Let's get to the bottom line.
- Here's what worked before.
- Based on past experience . . .
- The first step is ____; the second step is ____.
- Just tell me what needs to be done.
- Let's not reinvent the wheel.
- State the facts and only the facts.
- Let's get down to what's really important.
- I say we stick with what's tried-and-true.

How to Communicate with Oranges	
DO:	DON'T:
Begin the conversation on a positive note, pointing out the good things happening.	Ask them to do anything that's offensive or that will require them to be hurtful to other people.
Appreciate and recognize their efforts and contributions.	Interrupt them.
Encourage them to talk about their concerns.	Press them to make a decision before they have the chance to explore how they feel about it.
Be friendly and considerate of their feelings.	Put them in a position where they feel taken advantage of or put upon.
Honor your commitments to them.	Talk down to them or be condescending or patronizing.

How to Communicate with Oranges (cont'd)	
DO:	*DON'T:*
Always be polite and courteous.	Raise your voice.
Avoid offensive language.	Initiate confrontational conversations.
Appeal to their need to help.	Treat them impersonally.
Actively listen to what they're saying and be mindful of their body language.	Have them point out other people's inadequacies.
Be clear about what you need, especially if they're going to be responsible for providing it.	Talk about them behind their back.
Be attentive and relaxed.	
Begin by pointing out something positive they've done if you must criticize them.	
Ask them to share their feelings if you sense that you've stepped on their toes. Avoid letting them hold things inside.	
Avoid emotional confrontations.	
Use your own personal experiences as a means of making a point.	
Appeal to their need to be liked.	
Show a personal interest in them and ask about their family.	
Incorporate social activities in your interactions.	
Pay them sincere compliments, but don't go overboard.	

Phrases That Get Oranges' Attention

- Can you help me understand this?

- Here's my take the situation. How do you feel?

- What do you feel is the right thing to do?

- You have my word on it.

- Let's do whatever we need to in order to make you more comfortable.

- Do you feel that this will give you what you need?

- I'm having trouble getting through to _____. Would you talk to them?

- Would you help plan the annual sales meeting?

- I need someone to take care of this, and you're so good at that sort of thing.

- I need help getting others to support my idea.

- You're really good with people.

How to Communicate with Yellows	
DO:	**DON'T:**
Appeal to their need to know and understand.	Expect them to make a decision before they have time to think about the issue.
Appreciate their thoroughness and desire for perfection.	Present a problem if you don't want them to help solve it.
Keep in mind their sense of fairness and personal integrity.	Be repetitious or rehash a conversation.
Use words that stimulate their thinking.	Come across as a know-it-all.
Discuss possibilities with them.	Ask *why* questions, or they'll react emotionally (not good).
Ask them *what* questions so that they'll respond logically.	Become emotional.

How to Communicate with Yellows (cont'd)	
DO:	*DON'T:*
Be truthful and honest.	Expect them not to challenge want you're saying.
Solicit their suggestions and ideas.	Question their logic or tell them they're wrong.
Focus on the big picture.	Doubt their integrity.
Employ metaphors and analogies to make your point.	Hold them accountable for other people's inadequacies or mistakes.
Use words that engage their imagination.	Interrupt them.
Challenge their intellectual curiosity.	Try to one-up them.
Be organized and prepared and expect to be challenged.	Embarrass or humiliate them in front of others.
Consider both the cause and effect before presenting any change.	
Get to the point quickly.	
Offer bold, innovative approaches.	
Sell yourself as someone who's competent and self-confident.	
Tell them immediately if they hurt your feelings or offend you.	
Submit suggestions in writing first, because they need time to think things over.	
Be honest, direct, and straightforward.	
Resist the temptation to finish their sentences.	

How to Communicate with Yellows (cont'd)
DO:
Always expect them to ask questions.
Present several different options.
Be clear in what the objectives are and state them at the beginning of the conversation.

Phrases That Get Yellows' Attention

- What do you think the strategy should be?
- We need someone to take charge of this project. Are you interested?
- I need help solving a problem.
- What's wrong with this picture?
- Been there, done that. Let's come up with something new and exciting.
- What's your take on the situation?
- We need to figure out how to resolve these issues.
- Do you have any ideas?
- This may be a little off the wall, but what about . . . ?
- That's interesting; tell me more.
- I can't seem to get this thing to work. Can you help me?
- Let me bounce this idea off you.
- We need a new system to increase productivity.

How to Communicate with Greens	
DO:	*DON'T:*
Engage them in conversation by asking for their ideas.	Bog them down with details.
Allow the discussion to flow freely.	Silence or ignore them when they're expressing how they're feeling.
Show interest in them and their ideas.	Criticize or attack them personally. They'll go Red.
Appeal to their creativity.	Be sarcastic and disrespectful.
Use their name when speaking to them. It's music to their ears and personalizes the conversation.	Overwhelm them with rules.
Use metaphors and words that paint pictures.	Try to control the conversation if they're talking.
Allow them to ask questions.	Raise your voice or use threatening tones.
Keep conversations light, fun, and lively.	Treat them impersonally.
Share your ideas and dreams with them.	Dismiss, discount, or make light of their feelings.
Provide options and give them choices.	Micromanage them.
Smile and maintain good eye contact.	Take an authoritarian posture.
Acknowledge their feelings.	Laugh at their ideas.
Praise their efforts.	Embarrass them in front of their peers.
Present information in a way that appeals to their emotional and spiritual needs.	Dismiss their ideas before they have time to explain them.

How to Communicate with Greens (cont'd)	
DO:	*DON'T:*
Let your voice reflect your commitment and passion.	Curtail their need for social interaction.
Seek harmony and cooperation.	
Preface any criticism by telling them what they do well.	
Ask them to share their feelings.	
Show an interest in them and become their friend.	
Appeal to their desire to be unique.	
Always be sincere.	
Use words that are emotionally charged, such as *feel, care, happy, joy,* and *love.*	
Ask open-ended questions.	
Avoid confrontations.	
Compliment them.	
Be sensitive; they get their feelings hurt easily.	

Phrases That Get Greens' Attention

- What feels right to you?
- What's your intuition telling you?
- I love the way you create new ideas.
- You have a real talent for understanding people.
- Let's brainstorm to see if we can come up with something new.

- I'm not seeing where you're headed. Paint me a picture.
- What are your feelings about _____?
- You're always so warm, friendly, and positive.
- You have a very keen sense of what's going on.
- You sure know how to read people.
- Tell me the new and exciting things that are going on in your life.
- What have you done for fun lately?
- Let's talk about you.
- I'm not good at defusing conflict the way you are. Can you give me any ideas?
- I like the way you're always so willing to jump in.

> *"The greatest problem with communication*
> *is the <u>illusion</u> it has been achieved."*
> — attributed to George Bernard Shaw

Conflict Resolution

Conflict stems from personality differences and occurs when people don't see eye to eye, meaning that each person has a different perception of the same situation along with varying expectations of how the other parties should act. These problems often reflect power struggles that are occurring within a relationship, and the impetus behind them is the need for control. As a matter of fact, the greatest potential for trouble occurs when we're feeling out of control or if someone seems to have too much say over what we do. This is when we can really see how personality differences create incompatibility issues, which cause stress in our interactions. Here are the common conflict triggers by personality color:

What Causes Conflict to Occur

REDS

Wasting time, specifically their time

Not having their needs put first

Being taken advantage of

Losing at anything

Lazy, unproductive behavior

Inequity in responsibilities

Not getting their way

Disagreeing with them

Emotional outbursts

Lengthy explanations

YELLOWS

Not having the time to think through a decision

Making them look dumb or stupid

Questioning their decisions

False accusations

Being humiliated in front of other people

Doubting their integrity

Questioning their sense of responsibility

Being accountable for other people's mistakes

Dealing with emotional issues

Cutting them off when they're talking

ORANGES

Being treated impersonally

Insensitivity from others

Not being able to share feelings

Security being threatened

Being criticized

Not being appreciated

Accusations of being self-centered

Not being helped or supported with chores

GREENS

Not being taken seriously

Receiving criticism

Being ignored

Jealousy

Being suppressed and controlled

Getting told when to do something

Time constraints and restrictions

Being overly managed and directed

Common Conflict Behavior for Each Personality Color

REDS

Impatient, abrupt, and argumentative

Reactive, excitable, and easily angered

Controlling and demanding

Attack others personally

Micromanage people and tasks

YELLOWS

Tactless, argumentative, and aggressive

Distance themselves from people

Assume intellectual superiority over others

Challenge others' thinking and logic

Display emotional indifference

ORANGES

Go into avoidance and are overly accommodating

Worry, fret, and react emotionally

Become antagonistic and make sarcastic comments

Hold in emotions until the boiling point, then let loose

Emotionally controlling and manipulating

GREENS

Withdraw from interacting

Emotionally immobilized and submissive

Suppress feelings

Lose objectivity

Blame themselves for everything

How Anger Is Expressed When Conflict Occurs

REDS

Are more forceful

Become loud and use aggressive language

Pound fists and throw things

Physically domineering and demanding

Tactless and hurtful in what they say

Express disgust

YELLOWS

Become nitpicky and split hairs

Argumentative

Show open hostility and contempt

Verbose and challenging

Cold, indifferent stare

Express lack of trust

ORANGES

Become moody or silent

Yell and make vengeful, hurtful comments

Become emotionally exasperated

Moody outbursts

Antagonistic and sarcastic

Express disappointment

GREENS

Pout, brood, or cry

Bitter and hateful; express ultimatums

Shut down and give up trying

Become passive-aggressive

Fickle and unresponsive

Express disbelief

Using Power in a Conflict Situation

The use of power to get what we want is a natural part of our humanness, and we learn at a very early age how to apply it so that our basic needs are met. This can be obvious or subtle. Our motivation may be conscious (we're fully aware of why and how we're using it), or it can be subconscious (motivated by fears and emotional insecurities). Power can take on many forms and may intimidate, manipulate, coerce, seduce, influence, protect, control, silence, change minds, comfort, inspire, and motivate. Members of each personality color are most comfortable with different forms, especially in conflict situations.

Forms of Power Used by Each Personality Color

REDS	YELLOWS
Control	Superiority
Fear	Knowledge
Retribution	Intimidation
Rejection	Involvement
Physical intimidation	Mental manipulation

ORANGES	GREENS
Emotional manipulation	Emotional seduction
Silence	Tears
Blame	Guilt
Assertiveness	Submissiveness
Guilt	Helplessness

16 Steps to Resolving Conflict

1. Identify and define the situations creating the conflict.

2. Deal with issues, not personality differences.

3. Once the problems are defined, address them based on personality communication needs. In other words, speak the other person's language.

4. Examine the likely origin of the conflict: personal versus nonpersonal.

5. Set aside an appropriate time and place to discuss issues—somewhere neutral.

6. Ask everyone involved to express their feelings, thoughts, or concerns.

7. Don't allow blame to enter the conversation.

8. Ask each person involved to see the situation from the other parties' perspectives.

9. Request that everyone discuss their desired outcome.

10. List the alternatives and consequences.

11. Strive to reach solutions that will resolve the conflict so that everyone involved shares in the compromise.

12. Avoid words that make things personal, such as *you* or *your.*

13. Use calm voices to defuse the potential for emotional outbursts or hurt feelings.

14. Be sincere; don't patronize.

15. Ask questions.

16. Listen actively.

*"Conflict is the longest distance
between two different points of view."*
— Anonymous

▨ ▨ ▨

CHAPTER TEN

Time and
Task Management

Whether we agree that time equates to productivity or not, the fact is we all need some degree of scheduling in order to fulfill our basic human needs. Essentially, the structuring of time is a necessary part of our survival. It provides guidelines to help us fit in and adjust to the demands and expectations created by society. Simultaneously, it establishes the benchmarks needed to gauge our progress and mark the passage of life. When trying to understand how people relate to time and why they manage it in the ways they do, here are some key points to keep in mind:

- Everyone procrastinates when it comes to what their personality doesn't prefer, meaning that they'll avoid doing the things that cause them to function outside their true color.

- Each personality color has its own perception of time and how it should be used.

- Some colors control time, others adapt to it, and some don't want anything to do with it.

- Understanding a person's perception of time will help accommodate their needs. This will reduce stress for everyone.

- It's important to remember that no matter how much you try to get folks to comply with your perception of time, if they have different views, there are going to be problems.

- Effective time management should include some unscheduled periods.

- If dealing with time is creating undue stress, take a deep breath and ask yourself, *Will any of this really matter later on down the road?* If your answer is no, then you might want to reevaluate your priorities.

Four Different Perspectives of Time

There are basically four different perspectives of time, and all are determined by inherent personality traits. Because they're formed as a result of neurological wiring, one of these attitudes will surface very early on in each of us and will continue to influence how we value and use our time, no matter what our age or how much our conditioning tries to change it.

The Red Personality: Time Obsessive

Reds' obsession with time stems from an internal clock that instinctively drives everything they do. It's as if they're born with watches embedded in their wrists, another in their stomach, and a daily planner attached to the palms of their hands. Everything they do is driven by this element: time of day, month, and year.

If you ask Reds why they're so time conscious, they'll tell you that they become irritated when it's being wasted and feel out of control if they don't know where it's going. Their line of thinking is that if they manage things well and follow a tight schedule, then life will be productive and won't slip away from them. They also believe that this will eliminate confusion and lack of focus and allow them to channel their energy into producing the results they desire. Their motto regarding time is "Don't adapt to it—control it."

A Quick Glance at Reds' Perception of Time

- It's tangible.
- Once commitments are made, they're cast in concrete.
- Time is driven by the tasks at hand.
- It's measured by results.
- It equates to the bottom line.
- Now is all that exists—there's only the immediate to deal with.
- Time management is the only means to measure progress and ensure success.

How to Use This Information

- A rule of thumb when working or living with Reds is that when it comes to time, there are no generalities—only absolutes.

- When delegating a task, tell Reds exactly what needs to be done, along with your expectations, and give them a deadline. Then leave them alone. If they need more information or direction, they'll ask. You can always count on them to get the job done when expected.

- Don't try to control them. This won't enhance their productivity, nor will it create a cooperative team environment.

- Don't commit their time without their involvement or before gaining their agreement.

- Don't overload their schedules with your tasks or put them in the position of being accountable for your inability to manage time. It must have been a Red who said, "A lack of planning on your part doesn't constitute an emergency on my part."

- Don't hold open-ended meetings. If something is scheduled for an hour, then end it at 60 minutes. If you really want to win points with them, schedule a one-hour meeting and end it in 45 minutes. They'll see you as having your act together.

- Don't surprise them. If you know that there will be a change in the schedule, tell them as soon as you know, not at the last minute.

- If they procrastinate about doing something, it's usually because they don't want to do it.

The Orange Personality: Time Compulsive

While obsession and compulsion share many of the same behavioral characteristics, there's a major underlying motivational difference. The former is driven by individual needs, while the latter comes from other people. In the case of obsessive Reds, they're in control of their schedules, determining what they do and when they do it. This isn't true for compulsive individuals, who feel that someone else is in control; others' needs drive what they do and when. As a result, there's very little time—if any—for their own needs or to fit in their activities.

Welcome to the world of Oranges, whose time, lives, and activities always center on ensuring that everyone else's needs and demands are met emotionally and physically. As a matter of fact, taking care of and giving to others is their inherent nature, even when it means putting their own desires on the back burner. Oranges' schedules typically include running errands, juggling home and work, doing things that no one else wants to, and taking on more responsibility just because they have a hard time saying no. Consequently, they think that there's never enough time—and rightfully so, because just when they think that they have everything under control and can set aside a moment for themselves, someone else's needs pop up and any freedom they might have had suddenly disappears.

A Quick Glance at Oranges' Perception of Time

- It's relational and involves resolving people issues.

- It's based around individuals and fulfilling their needs.

- Scheduling restrictions are used as a means of controlling others.

- Time is measured by the quality of their relationships.

- Commitments mean doing what others say they're going to do.

- Time usage is determined by how they feel.

- Their days are best spent interacting with people.

How to Use This Information

- Alleviate their worries by explaining what's going on. Remember that they have a low-level anxiety about the unknown and how it will impact their time.

- Give them the time they need to make decisions, and don't press them to do something that doesn't feel right.

- If you don't have the time to listen, then don't ask how they're doing.

- Avoid overloading their schedule, as it's already full from trying to meet other people's needs.

- If you need their help, begin by asking if they have time.

- Remember that if they're pressed for time, they'll tend to be emotionally reactive.

- Don't impose your deadlines on them just because you didn't plan well.

- When you give them tasks, include timelines and then leave them alone.

- Don't take advantage of their not being able to say no.

- Jump in and help them if there's a people problem because they procrastinate when dealing with these issues. They'd rather spend time being supportive and making sure that everyone has what they need to do the job.

The Yellow Personality: Time Imperative

Yellows' perception of time is that there's never enough of it. They perpetually find tasks exceeding the time allotted, and their favorite saying is "Work expands to exceed the time needed, whether it's available or not." Members of this color live with a never-ending to-do list that's like a continuous loop. At least with a list, you start at the top and work your way to the bottom; then when you've completed the last task, you're done. Not so for the Yellow—they're never finished because their tasks don't have a beginning or an end. The items just keep recycling and are continually being added to.

As a matter of fact, being done isn't even an option, as far as they're concerned. The issue for Yellows is that while they're doing one thing, their minds are thinking about another and another and another. To help compensate for this, they develop a mental prioritization process at a very early age that's continually evaluating all tasks, determining their degree of urgency, and reprioritizing them. It's this sequence that drives their time-imperative perspective.

A Quick Glance at Yellows' Perception of Time

- It equates to productivity.
- It's a resource to be fully utilized.
- It's relative.
- It's measured in tasks rather than events.
- It isn't cast in concrete.
- It's conceptual.
- It's impersonal.

How to Use This Information

- Give them the time they need to think things through.

- Don't commit their time without involving them in the decision.

- Don't fill their schedules so much that they don't have discretionary periods.

- Be punctual; don't keep Yellows waiting.

- Don't blindside them with your deadlines.

- If you need their attention and they're in the middle of something, give them the time to mentally shift gears.

- Involve them in the planning process so that they can organize their schedules.

- They'll avoid getting started on something until *how* to do it firmly gels in their mind. Help expedite this process by giving them the information they need and letting them know whether there's a deadline.

- They'll procrastinate if they don't want to do a particular job. If you notice this, ask them, "Is this something you want to do or shall I get someone else to do it?" If they say that they'll handle it, drop it and don't push them. They'll eventually get it done.

The Green Personality: Time Impulsive

Greens' lives center on experiences and social interactions. Consequently, they don't like to schedule their time so tightly that they can't be spontaneous and take advantage of whatever comes their way. Spur-of-the-moment is how they prefer to live, and in fact, they see rigid structure as a major deterrent to the quality of their lives. They want to be able to go with the flow, change plans without hesitation, and be prepared to do the totally unexpected.

Greens enjoy the unpredictability of life and want to have the freedom to engage in whatever surprises it offers. After all, from their perspective, that's what makes life exciting and gives it meaning. They truly believe that if they aren't flexible, they might miss an opportunity when it comes knocking at their door. It's this perspective that drives their time-impulsive behavior significantly.

Now, this isn't to imply that Greens can't manage their schedules, because they're very good at doing so when it's important to them—meaning when they're doing something they want to do. Yet even when that's the case, if something better comes along, they'll drop everything and go. They figure that they can always come back, even if it means working all night to get the job done or hit a deadline.

Greens struggle with time the most when someone else tries to control their activities and tells them how to manage their time. Should they find themselves in this situation, they'll become rebellious and feel trapped. They'll cop a "don't give a damn" attitude and decide that it's your problem, not theirs, so you should deal with it—or else they'll go into their Red emotional outburst and point out your personal shortcomings.

Time isn't literal for Greens. A couple of minutes for another color can range anywhere from minutes to hours for them; and scheduling should be an option, rather than an edict.

A Quick Glance at Greens' Perception of Time

- It's a moving target.

- It can be adapted to fit any unforeseen circumstances.

- They should be evaluated on their efforts in a particular period of time, not on the bottom line.

- Time is often overscheduled.

- Time is well spent if they're sharing experiences with other people.

- They must have time for play.

- Time is emotional.

How to Use This Information

- If Greens are involved in a task with a deadline, give them a false date, perhaps a day or two before the project is actually due. This way they can hit the real deadline and feel good about themselves.

- Don't control their activities or make them accountable for every minute.

- They're easily distracted from the tasks at hand, so check on their progress regularly to be sure they're getting the job done.

- Their relationship with time is different from the other personality colors, so understand that they have a tendency to "putter away" their days.

- They believe that they always have time to do one more thing.

- If they tell you they'll be right with you, don't take it literally—expect it to be at least several minutes or more.

- They're chronically late, so plan accordingly.

- Their pattern is to wait until the last minute to plan things, as this gives them the flexibility to change their minds if they need to. If having everything worked out ahead of time is important to you, then you'd better do it yourself.

- They procrastinate when it comes to getting organized, because they'd rather spend their time doing something else. When they appear to have their affairs in order, notice it and be supportive.

Task Management

Before managers can do their work, there must be a list of jobs to be completed and people to do the work. The key to managing resources effectively lies in knowing how to match the employees with the tasks to maximize productivity and minimize frustration and stress for everyone. When this happens, everything gets done and everyone enjoys success. Here are some motivations, qualities, and limitations by color that may be helpful in determining which personality might be most suitable for a particular job.

Using Personality Color in Task Assignment

Reds: Task Oriented

- Loyal, steadfast, and strongly committed to the employer and organization
- Follow procedures and directions readily
- High tolerance for repetition
- Motivated and excited by competitive challenges
- Resistant to change for its own sake
- Work well in a chain-of-command hierarchy
- Make good team leaders
- Natural task managers
- Prefer established ways of doing things
- "Get it done now" attitude
- Need structure and organization
- Require tasks to be clearly defined
- Strong willed, dogmatic, and focused
- Would rather use existing skills than take the time to learn new ones
- Avoid problems and tasks that are too complex
- Strong work ethic and high expectations of themselves and others
- Aggressive and demanding
- Motivated by the bottom line
- Deadline oriented

Oranges: People Oriented

- Good interpersonal skills
- Excellent at detail management and administering control processes

- Follow procedures and directions readily
- High tolerance for repetition
- Motivated by relationships and supportive environments
- Accept change when it enhances the quality of their group's work situation
- Work well in a chain-of-command hierarchy
- Make good team members
- Expect cooperation and work toward common goals of their group
- Need people interaction
- Natural organizers
- Warm, friendly, and considerate
- Need direct supervision, yet not close management

Yellows: Task Oriented

- Instinctively innovative and resourceful
- Dislike repetition
- Thrive on a steady diet of productivity enhancements and procedural changes
- Motivated by challenging opportunities that demand creative solutions
- Accept change readily if it's well thought out and administered
- Continually questioning and challenging perceived illogical management decisions
- Prefer an open-dialogue environment rather than a rigid chain of command
- Contribute significantly to team activities when their input is welcomed and respected

- Independent conceptual thinkers
- Devise new systems for adapting group functions
- Work well alone; don't need interaction with others
- Perfectionists and workaholics
- Natural leaders
- Impatient with details
- Skilled strategists and troubleshooters

Greens: People Oriented

- Work to live; don't live to work
- Dislike repetition
- Want to be in an environment where group interaction and sociability are the norm
- Don't like deadlines or following rigid procedures
- Motivated by creative stimulation and personal recognition
- Accept regular change as the ideal environment in which to work
- Prefer an open-dialogue environment and nondirective management
- Make good team members when they can stay focused on the group's objectives
- Emotionally sensitive; get feelings hurt easily
- Avoid conflict and dealing with unpleasant situations or people
- Inspiring and enthusiastic leaders
- Would rather create than facilitate
- Excel in people management, not dealing with details
- Strong advocates for people's rights
- Need freedom to express emotions

*Square pegs in round holes work
no better than round pegs in square holes.*

▩   ▩   ▩

CHAPTER ELEVEN

Problem Solving

The problem with problem solving is that each color sees the others as being the problem, especially when having to deal with conflict in a group situation. However, if they can all recognize each color's unique contribution, it will be easier to overlook the differences and come up with solutions that will satisfy everyone's needs. The fact is, the more colors involved in solving a problem, the better balanced the solution, the greater the group commitment to the outcome, and the more profitable the end results. Understanding differences and harnessing each color's problem-solving strengths is a win-win for all parties. Here are some suggestions that can help make the process more effective.

Reds' Problem-Solving Style: Just Give Me the Facts

Reds carefully evaluate each step and the facts before moving on. They don't jump around or take shortcuts in their mental processing. They write down each necessary action, identify who's responsible, assign a timeline, and then go on to the next step. This process gives them the means to measure progress, as well as a method for double-checking from time to time to see if the decision they made is still the right one. Their problem-solving style includes these steps:

1. Initiate an orderly and sequential procedure for gathering and analyzing all relevant information.

2. Determine what or who caused the problem and then quickly move into action to eliminate this source.

3. Establish mental constraints regarding what's acceptable or not, and what's practicable or not.

4. Rule out options (sometimes prematurely) that can't be verified by proven experience or justified with a preconceived implementation plan.

5. Compare alternative solutions to one another and weigh their respective merits by listing all the events that should happen, assigning probabilities and financial consequences to each possibility. This approach allows Reds to choose an optimal course of action.

6. Find ways to make task management simpler, faster, and more productive.

7. Rely on the group's historical averages or top management's planned levels of performance standards as guidelines for determining solutions.

8. Use their step-by-step processing as filters so that they can quickly narrow problems down to such

relevant factors as what, when, where, and how the decision will affect the organization.

9. Identify ways to cut through red tape in order to achieve a timely and satisfactory solution.

10. Establish themselves as the central point for information clarification, dissemination, and exchange in order to assure unity of command and consistency of approach.

11. Derive the maximum number of interpretations and possible solutions from the same information.

12. Once they've mentally reached a solution, they'll announce the decision boldly and expect everyone involved to start the implementation process immediately. In Reds' minds, their decision is the final word.

13. Reluctantly set aside work in progress in order to respond to changes in the organization's direction, bottlenecks in work flow, or management crises.

14. If pressed, they'll come up with solutions too quickly and won't take the time necessary to process facts step-by-step. Consequently, they may end up living with decisions that are less than desirable.

How to Use This Information When Working with Reds

- Explain the problem in very specific terms, including all known facts and details and any history associated with the issue. Identify how it's affecting the organization.

- When discussing the subject in a meeting, remind people to keep it short, simple, and to the point. No brainstorming or speculating.

- Clearly explain what needs to be done and what you expect from them.

- Avoid lengthy explanations and sharing feelings.

- Once a solution has been agreed upon, don't continue to rehash it.

- Make sure that they walk away with an action plan and a deadline.

Oranges' Problem-Solving Style: Let's All Agree

Oranges also follow a step-by-step process in working toward a solution. Unlike Reds, however, who rely strictly on facts, these folks incorporate facts, emotional undertones, and other external input. They use a teamwork approach, asking for advice from anyone who will be impacted by their decisions. Once they receive the feedback they need, they apply it to each of their steps to ensure that there's a good match. If there isn't for any reason, Oranges will go back and reevaluate the problem and create new steps; they'll keep starting over until they get a group consensus. They'll always seek solutions in which all people involved will benefit equally. Their method includes these steps:

1. Review and often retain voluminous piles of memos, reports, and files to ensure the accuracy of information and the proper chronology of events.

2. Solicit the feelings and views of others rather than relying on their personal observations.

3. Create committees to collect facts and make recommendations when confronted with issues that will affect the organizational structure.

4. Compare people's experiences as a means of sorting facts from opinions.

5. Base decisions on conventional standards of conduct; endorse incremental rather than radical changes.

6. Collect information in a matter-of-fact and unbiased manner from virtually everyone affected by or experienced with the issue and from all the witnesses to that particular problem.

7. Recount every exchange of dialogue, describing each fact in detail when reporting the events observed or incidents they were involved in.

8. React submissively when they feel that they're being personally attacked.

9. Allow their positions and perspectives to be influenced by anyone they have a relationship with or those who have been sincere, cooperative, and open.

10. View problems as disruptions affecting their schedules and routines.

11. Consider and respect the opinions of other people without asking them to compromise their values.

12. Defer any problems that affect the company to their superiors.

13. Focus on finding solutions that will reconcile differences between people.

How to Use This Information When Working with Oranges

-   Stress how the problem is affecting people within the organization and how the solution will address morale issues.

-   Allow them to express their concerns and feelings. Don't silence or discredit them.

-   Express the importance of sharing personal values, but if necessary, remind them that their opinions shouldn't cloud the issues.

- Be sensitive to how the problems are being explained: Watch tones of voice and body language, stick to the issue, and avoid any comments that could be interpreted as personal attacks.

- Listen, listen, and listen some more. Don't tune them out, because they have the emotional pulse of the organization.

- Explain how they can help and draw on their people skills to get others to buy into the solution. They're great ambassadors for creating team efforts.

Yellows' Problem-Solving Style: Think It Through and Do It Right

Yellows are capable of grasping all parts of a problem quickly and simultaneously integrating a step-by-step process with the randomness offered by the right frontal quadrant. They evaluate facts, explore possibilities, juggle outcomes, play out scenarios, and assess causes and effects while remaining open to new solutions. They view problems as puzzles and seek the best and most efficient way to figure them out. They enjoy challenges—the more complex the problem, the better they perform. Their problem-solving style includes these steps:

1. Create scenarios of what's likely to happen if the recommended decision is accepted and implemented, including what might be done to change the outcome if they encounter obstacles, resistance, or undesirable side effects.

2. Envision the ideal criteria for decisions and compare the specific attributes of each alternative to this standard before accepting compromises, adaptations, or shortcuts.

3. Conceptually explore alternatives, often abandoning ideas, backtracking, and redefining their personal understanding of the problem itself.

4. Speculate (as if thinking aloud) about the possibilities as a means of evoking a variety of solutions drawn from their personal "idea files."

5. Insist on knowing, questioning, and debating the causes, dynamics, or implications of things—often to the point of hairsplitting and challenging authority.

6. Conceptualize the prospects for novel applications and alternatives. They'll even manipulate facts and redirect information in order to open up new possibilities.

7. Treat individual problems as symptoms of much larger, systemic problems and connect the current events to an overall trend.

8. Evaluate the basic functions of products or services, assess their relative impact, and identify changes that would increase the value or improve the return on investment.

9. Compare organizational performance against changing needs or state-of-the-art knowledge and convert the differences into challenging but attainable objectives that act as guides to improve both performance and productivity.

10. Involve themselves more in solving problems rather than following through on decisions.

How to Use This Information
When Working with Yellows

- Acknowledge their ability to provide innovative yet practical solutions.

- State the problem clearly, but don't go into a lot of detail or tell them how they should try to solve it. Leave them alone to work out the solution.

- Don't press them for answers in a meeting. Instead, give them time to think. If they come up with something, they'll share their thoughts.

- At all times, keep the objectives clear in everyone's minds to discourage others from personalizing things.

- When a solution is presented, be sure it's thoroughly explored before moving on to the next issue. Don't jump around.

- Don't openly criticize their ideas or interrupt them. They'll disengage and become indifferent.

Greens' Problem-Solving Style:
Don't Bother Me—I'm Creating

Rather than a methodical, sequential processing of information, Greens prefer to randomly process information, because this lets them explore all the possibilities. Their holistic perspective allows them to look at the overall picture and thereby come up with a variety of solutions, some of which are viable.

They think that if they can conceive a solution and believe it will work, then they'll be able to achieve the results they want. However, if you were to ask them for their plan of action, they'd be hard-pressed to tell you, because they view the entire undertaking as very fluid. Greens figure that if they want something badly enough and put it out there in the universe, it will take care of itself. The problem they run into is that this randomness means they have a difficult time knowing where to start and when to finish, because the solution is just part of the process instead of the final destination. Related to this is their perspective that problem-solving is ongoing, so they measure their progress on effort and not on the bottom line. Their problem-solving style includes these steps:

1. Ask the people who will be affected by the decisions to prepare their positions privately, then explain them in group sessions. At these meetings, they'll discuss each idea, brainstorm solutions, rank the options, and ultimately select the best one based on group consensus.

2. Place a greater value on how choices will affect people emotionally rather than whether things are good for the company.

3. Allow their conclusions to be influenced by the likes and dislikes of others, especially their friends.

4. Evaluate solutions based on whether they'll satisfy everyone's needs. They'll reject anything intended to serve individuals rather than the group.

5. Raise idea-generating questions to engage people in the decision-making process and produce a variety of solutions, some more original than others, but none necessarily more correct.

6. Use metaphors and analogies to conceptualize relationships between the obvious and the obscure and to understand the interconnectedness between problems and solutions.

7. Look for ways to back out of decisions they've already made, especially if those choices don't meet their personal needs or if there's a chance that they'll end up in a conflict-charged environment.

8. Encourage brainstorming activities as part of the evaluation process and for creating new ideas.

9. Voice concerns over lack of sensitivity regarding the feelings of those involved in the decision-making process. They're also concerned about anyone being treated impersonally.

10. Attend personal- and professional-development workshops so that they can become more effective

in communicating their ideas and working with others.

11. Rely on hunches, gut feelings, and intuitive insight for direction.

12. Consider all emotional implications before coming to a conclusion, then leave their options open just in case something better comes along.

How to Use This Information When Working with Greens

• Recognize that they become overwhelmed with too many facts and begin to daydream. The result is that they won't participate in the process.

• Encourage brainstorming to identify as many solutions as possible. This is just idea dumping for Greens, so don't criticize their ideas or place rules on the process.

• Understand that they'll offer concepts instead of facts, and possibilities rather than solutions. They'll be more interested in creating ideas than implementing them.

• Have an agenda and stick to it while factoring in their need to talk, voice their opinions, and explore possibilities.

• Encourage them to share their feelings, but don't let meetings become gripe sessions.

- Staying grounded and being present in the moment aren't their strengths. However, if you make the problem-solving process fun and exciting, they'll stay engaged.

Problem-Solving Quick-Reference Guide

REDS

Stick with what's familiar

Make decisions quickly based on facts

See problems as being black or white

Rely on historical precedent

Seek immediate solutions

YELLOWS

Look for innovative, untried solutions

Require time to think and analyze options

See problems as complex and having variables

Rely on ingenuity and intelligence

Seek both immediate and long-term solutions

ORANGES

Solicit others' opinions

Are influenced by emotions

Evaluate personal impact

Seek incremental changes

Create solutions based on others' perspectives

GREENS

Solicit others' positions and perspectives

Are influenced by intuition and imagination

Evaluate team impact

Encourage total change

Create solutions based on their own perspectives

Learning Styles Quick-Reference Guide

REDS

Initiate the learning process externally

Auditory, conceptual, visual, and kinesthetic

Prefer a practical application of ideas

Exacting, emphasizing quality and productivity

Pragmatic and realistic

Thrive on planning and timelines

YELLOWS

Initiate the learning process internally

Conceptual, visual, kinesthetic, and auditory

Create concepts and solutions

Lead by principles and procedures

Accurate and knowledgeable

Thrive on challenges and crisis

ORANGES

Initiate the learning process externally

Auditory, kinesthetic, visual, and conceptual

Build relationships

Interested in cooperative efforts

Caring and sensitive

Thrive on social interaction

GREENS

Initiate the learning process externally

Visual, kinesthetic, auditory, and conceptual

Create new ideas

Help people become more self-aware

Inspiring and helpful

Thrive on experiencing something new

If you can remember that everything people do is based on perception, it will be easier for you to understand why everyone sees problems differently, and their decisions aren't necessarily those you'd make. These varying viewpoints also determine everyone's ability to learn and what they're interested in, so each of the four personality colors learns differently. Keeping this in mind will make it easier for you to create a working environment where being productive and learning go hand in hand. If you know employees' personality colors, decision-making styles, and how they learn, then you'll be more effective as both a manager and teacher.

Finally, there are basically two ways to deal with problems. The first relies on the idea that any issue can be handled if you invest unlimited time or money. The second is based on the idea that anything can be solved better if you harness the styles of each of the personality types to gain four-color acceptance and perception.

Once defined and clarified, a problem is half solved.

※　※　※

CHAPTER TWELVE

Team Building

In attempting to reach top performance, successful teams face many challenges. The first and foremost is how to deal with personality differences. Confronting obstacles, solving problems, and assimilating changes can strengthen the organization if everyone understands what each individual brings to the table and how to manage issues rather than succumb to personal attacks. Here are some of the fundamental contributors to success:

— **Purpose** creates focus, identifies objectives, and helps build confidence. Without this quality, the team has no sense of direction and can't harness its efforts toward reaching the desired results.

— **Process** establishes the action plan, methods, and systems. It sets the benchmarks needed for staff members to understand how they're going to be measured and their role in achieving the objectives.

— **Communication** is more than just talking and telling. It also includes listening and is the vehicle used for conveying trust, appreciation, and approval. This process is both verbal and nonverbal.

— **Involvement** ensures that everyone participates and works cooperatively toward achieving a common purpose. It includes:

- Asking team members, management, and product vendors how they can each contribute to the achievement of the purpose

- Soliciting ideas, suggestions, and concerns from every person in the group

- Matching individual skills and motivation with assignments

— **Trust** is the foundation upon which effective teams are built. It provides the stability and security that workers need to feel safe when sharing their emotions and the assurance that everyone will follow through.

— **Commitment** is fostered by trust, and it involves getting each staff member to buy into giving 100 percent to both the team and its purpose. When this quality exists, people keep their word in a timely manner. It means putting the needs of the individual aside and focusing on the good of the group.

Team Contributions by Personality Color

REDS

Detail oriented

Predictable and realistic

Excel in managing processes and tasks

Implement action plans

Structured and organized

Conscientious

Competitive

Responsible and helpful

YELLOWS

Solution oriented

Exhibit expertise and competency

Develop processes and systems

Create action plans

Innovative

Self-confident

Focused on objectives

Strategist and troubleshooter

ORANGES

Relationship oriented

Effective at getting people involved

Cooperative

Patient with routine and redundancy

Create supportive environments

Administer action plans

Sensitive and caring

Avoid conflict

GREENS

Team oriented

Masterful at coming up with ideas

Creative

Dislike routine

Create social environments

Facilitate action plans

Agreeable and easygoing

Resolve conflict

Six Common Team Pitfalls

Recognizing the warning signals that there's a problem within the team is critical to achieving peak performance.

Here are six warning signs that managers should be aware of, along with their causes and symptoms:

1. **Burnout:** tension, signs of work overload, frustration, lack of focus

2. **Conflict:** personality differences, inequitable allocation of workloads, preferential treatment

3. **Complacency:** resting on laurels, avoiding taking action, procrastination

4. **Leadership dependency:** resistance to taking initiative or making decisions without leader's approval, trying to push problems up the chain of command

5. **Elitism:** arrogance, always thinking their ideas are better than others, resistance to listening, disregarding feedback

6. **Group consciousness:** no conflict, no misunderstandings, always wanting to please, going with the flow

The Six Common Pitfalls by Personality Color

1. **Burnout:** Reds
2. **Conflict:** Reds and Oranges
3. **Complacency:** Greens
4. **Leadership dependency:** Oranges
5. **Elitism:** Yellows
6. **Group consciousness:** Oranges and Greens

Tips for Building Successful Teams

- Be sure that the personality types represented in the group are the best ones to get the job done.

- Include all four colors.

- Clearly define job responsibilities and match personality types with assignments.

- Set up tracking systems and regularly monitor the group's progress.

- Identify problems and deal with them quickly, before they affect overall productivity.

- Figure out who will be responsible for determining when the objective has been reached.

- Create an environment where every person's input is valued.

Synergism requires a four-color team.

※ ※ ※

CHAPTER THIRTEEN

How Each Color Sees the Others

How each personality sees the others depends on where the viewers are at that particular moment. If they're feeling good about themselves and are in an upbeat, productive frame of mind, then the other colors are going to be seen from the same positive perspective. The result is a higher degree of tolerance for differences. However, if people are stressed, then they're more likely to see their interactions as being negative. If you can remember that how you see the other colors begins with you—it's a lot easier to get along with people and achieve your desired results.

How Reds Perceive Other Personalities

How Reds See Reds

Positive	Negative
Good providers	Controlling
Challenging competitors	Poor losers
Reliable and responsible	Unpredictable and irresponsible
Easygoing	Temperamental
Productive and effective	Demanding and ineffective

Supportive and helpful	Self-centered
Realistic	Dogmatic
Organized	Out of control
Objective and open-minded	Stubborn and unrealistic
Accepting and tolerant	Intolerant

How Reds See Oranges

Positive	Negative
Cooperative	Emotionally demanding
Happy and easygoing	Uptight and difficult to get along with
Emotionally sensitive	Emotionally volatile
Predictable and reliable	Unreasonable
Socially adept	Bossy
Good caretakers	Self-centered
Hardworking	Resentful and unappreciative
Loving and gentle	Moody and spiteful
Supportive	Stubborn
Happy	Never satisfied

How Reds See Yellows

Positive	Negative
Innovative	Unrealistic
Logical	Theoretical
Easy to get along with	Aloof and impersonal
Intelligent and knowledgeable	Impractical and self-absorbed
Self-confident	Arrogant

Serious   Resistant
Challenging   Troublemakers
Team players   Nonconformists
Competent   Complicated
Supportive   Incorrigible

How Reds See Greens

Positive	**Negative**
Risk takers	Foolish
Spontaneous	Irresponsible
Agreeable	Volatile
Creative	Loose cannons
Fun	Flighty
Up for anything	Impractical
Visionaries	Dreamers
Emotionally sensitive	Emotionally complicated
Easygoing	Undermining

How Oranges Perceive Other Personalities

How Oranges See Reds

Positive	**Negative**
Good providers	Self-centered
Aggressive	Domineering
Strong and opinionated	Demanding
Organized	Obsessive
Intelligent	Self-absorbed

Supportive and helpful	Pensive and inflexible
Predictable	Unreliable
Task driven	Never pleased
Cooperative	Selfish

How Oranges See Oranges

Positive	Negative
Dependable and cooperative	Domineering and bossy
Considerate	Insensitive
Accommodating	Dictatorial
Trustworthy	Gossipy
Emotionally sensitive	Fickle
Supportive	Demanding
Social	Controlling
Friendly	Judgmental
Loyal	Untrustworthy

How Oranges See Yellows

Positive	Negative
Good idea people	Unrealistic
Reliable	Unpredictable
Leaders	Egotistical
Helpful	Elitists
Predictable	Uncooperative
Professional	Cold and indifferent
Sensitive	Unforgiving
Caring	Insensitive
Straightforward	Rude

How Oranges See Greens

Positive	Negative
Spontaneous	Irresponsible
Nurturing	Self-absorbed
Easygoing	Procrastinating
Flexible	Indecisive
Laid-back	Lazy
Friendly	Fickle
Chatty	Chatterboxes
Carefree	Chronically late
Emotionally approachable	Unpredictable

How Yellows Perceive Other Personalities

How Yellows See Reds

Positive	Negative
Reliable and organized	Rigid and unimaginative
Good task managers	Dogmatic
Detail oriented	Limited in their perspective
Predictable	Inflexible
Supportive	Demanding
Realistic	Not visionary
Dependable	Controlling
Cooperative	Egotistical
Bottom-line oriented	Combative

How Yellows See Oranges

Positive	Negative
Sensitive	Emotionally volatile
Caring	Self-absorbed
Cooperative	Demanding
Supportive	Moody and pensive
Helpful	Manipulative
Dependable	Self-serving
Predictable	Fickle
Trustworthy	Unpredictable
Consistent	Temperamental

How Yellows See Yellows

Positive	Negative
Visionaries	Hairsplitting
Compatible	Tactless
Strategic	Meddling
Productive	Procrastinators
Intelligent	Manipulative
Self-confident	Stuffy
Cooperative	Intolerant
Reliable	Contentious
Serious	Argumentative
Focused	Pushy

How Yellows See Greens

Positive	Negative
Spontaneous	Tardy
Easygoing	Unrealistic
Enthusiastic	Scattered
Flexible and adaptable	Myopic
Creative	Unreliable
Gregarious	Emotionally volatile
Convincing	Undisciplined
Motivating	Inconsistent
Personable	Self-absorbed
Supportive	Indecisive

How Greens Perceive Other Personalities

How Greens See Reds

Positive	Negative
Good providers	Domineering
Steady	Controlling
Predictable	Self-serving
Industrious	Dogmatic
Stable	Demanding
Focused	Rigid
Conscientious	Verbally abusive
Intense	Uncooperative
Competitive	Explosive
Supportive	Unimaginative
Reliable	Insensitive

How Greens See Oranges

Positive	Negative
Sensitive	Unimaginative
Dependable	Controlling
Helpful	Self-centered
Caring	Overbearing
Responsible	Inflexible
Sympathetic	Serious
Compassionate	Overly protective
Friendly	Emotional
Good judgment	Histrionic

How Greens See Yellows

Positive	Negative
Interesting	Harsh
Visionaries	Insensitive
Planners	Impersonal
Problem solvers	Stoic
Predictable	Overly critical
Dependable	Judgmental
Intelligent	Intolerant
Nonconformists	Narrow-minded
Competent	Unrelenting
Knowledgeable	Stubborn
Effective	Too serious

How Greens See Greens

Positive	Negative
Fun	Scattered
Playful	Spiteful
Sensitive	Critical
Exciting	Shallow
Cooperative	Jealous
Joyful	Lacking focus
Stimulating	Intolerant
Lighthearted	Undisciplined
Easygoing	Moody
Open and receptive	Fickle
Optimistic	Undependable
Empathetic	Pessimistic
Forgiving	Explosive

Each one of us is unique, just like everyone else.

⁂

Afterword

While this book has focused on understanding personality in order to manage other people more effectively, it's also been an opportunity for you to learn more about who you are and why you do the things you do.

I've discovered from years of teaching how personality impacts every aspect of our lives—and that the greatest gift is to discover who we really are. The ancient philosophers of Greece counseled *Know thyself,* for they believed that only then was it possible to manifest the soul's desires and to heal what ails the body, mind, and spirit. These great teachers of human behavior reminded their students that if they remained dependent upon other people's thoughts and perceptions, they limited what they were capable of achieving and what they could become. Rather than succumbing to this fate, they advocated freedom from false personalities in order to create a better life—one that supported getting where they wanted to go and doing what they wanted to do.

I, too, believe that the only way to be truly successful in life is to know yourself, for this is how you discover your inherent strengths; eliminate situations where you function from your weaknesses; and create the experiences, relationships, and environments that make it possible for you to go from where you are to where you want to be.

I'd like to conclude this book by sharing the attributes of successful people that apply to all four colors:

1. They're perennial observers of human behavior, both their own and that of others.

2. They believe that they alone are responsible for their lives.

3. They know they have a purpose and continually seek new experiences that will help them discover what it is.

4. They embrace their uniqueness and wear it like a badge of honor.

5. They understand the power of thought and use it to manifest what they desire.

6. They believe in themselves.

7. They see opportunity in every obstacle and growth in every challenge.

8. They exceed their personal expectations and avoid unrealistic expectations.

9. They understand the importance of self-forgiveness.

10. They live a life of significance by giving more than they take.

Thomas Edison once said, "If we did all of the things we are capable of doing, we would literally astound ourselves." I say, "If we could see the magnificence of who we are through the eyes of our personality, we'd never question what we're capable of achieving."

How about starting to create the life you desire today?

※　※　※

Acknowledgments

A book is typically not the creation of one person, but the product of many individuals and their willingness to share who they are. It's brought to life through the contribution of a rainbow of personality colors that make up our world. This project is the result of many wonderful people who contributed stories of their management successes and failures and have offered their perspectives, opened up their hearts, and shown their true colors to add credibility and diversified perspectives. What I've learned over the years of studying, researching, and sharing information about personality is that it's not only an integral part of who we are, but it's also a vital part of how we work, interact, and live with each other. My thanks to all of you, for you showed me through your words and deeds what the art of management is really all about.

There are a number of people who stand out and whom I'd like to acknowledge. First and foremost is my husband, Bruce, for he not only drew upon his many years as a successful manager, but he actually co-authored this book with me. Our process of working together as two Yellows was a magical experience, for we share a deep and loving bond with each other, as well as being the best of friends. However, we never realized how closely we were aligned in our thinking. Talk about teamwork! When I got stuck with words, he stepped in and picked up where I left off without even reading what I'd written. Thank you for making this book come to life and for helping me discover more about how we really are two of a kind.

Thank you to Diana and Floyd Haas, my Green daughter and Yellow son-in-law. Both of you are eminently gifted in what you bring to the business world with your understanding of personality and sensitivity to the differences in people. Your employers are lucky to have you on their teams, for your ethics and loyalty are inspirational, and your contributions to their success are significant.

Bill Klein (Red), you're a manager extraordinaire, and I thank you for your support of my work and your contributions. Your insight and feedback was of great value. I hope you enjoy the book! And Helene Van Sant-Klein (Green), your perspective on dealing with Reds was invaluable. Your warm, caring friendship and your sensitivity make my heart smile. Thanks to both of you for being in my life, which is much richer because of you.

Others I would like to thank include Naomi Aoyagi (Orange), Chari Wurtzel (Yellow), Bob Franke (Red), Gayle Dax-Conroy (Yellow), Tracy Flynn-Bowe (Yellow), Bob Eoss (Red), and Jeanie Bennett (Yellow). You're remarkable mentors and friends.

Thanks to Reid Tracy, Jill Kramer, Shannon Littrell, Jessica Vermooten, Charles McStravick, and all the Hay House staff for your support of my work. Hay House has been a wonderful gift in my life and responsible for making my dreams of being an author come true.

Finally, thanks to my clients and students of all colors who so lovingly assisted me in my research by letting me become a part of your lives. I am deeply indebted to all of you, for without your being who you are, I wouldn't have the understanding of personality that I do, nor would I have had the pleasure of learning about that inherent part of us that drives and enriches us all.

※　※　※

About the Author

Carol Ritberger, Ph.D., medical intuitive, is an innovative leader in the fields of personality typology and intuitive medicine. She has devoted more than 25 years to researching the impact of stress, emotions, and personality type on the health and well-being of the physical body. Carol holds two doctorates, one in religious philosophy and the other in esoteric philosophy and hermetic sciences. Her works include *Your Personality, Your Health; What Color Is Your Personality?;* and *Love . . . What's Personality Got to Do with It?,* all of which have received national recognition for their innovative approach to self-help; and she has been featured in *Good Housekeeping, Yoga Journal, Woman's World, Men's Health, GQ,* and *Healthy Living.* She has appeared on television programs such as *Extra, Healthy Living,* and *New Attitudes,* as well as on many national radio shows.

Carol is the executive director of The Ritberger Institute, which offers personal and professional development programs. Its goal is to assist its students in accessing and developing their intuition for business, personal, and spiritual growth. It offers an array of classes, including personality training and certification and intuitive-medicine programs.

Carol lives in Northern California with her husband, Bruce, with whom she cofounded The Ritberger Institute.

For more information on programs and presentations offered through the institute, please visit her Website: **www.ritberger.com**.

※　※　※

We hope you enjoyed this Hay House book. If you'd like to receive our online catalog featuring additional information on Hay House books and products, or if you'd like to find out more about the Hay Foundation, please contact:

Hay House, Inc., P.O. Box 5100, Carlsbad, CA 92018-5100
(760) 431-7695 or (800) 654-5126
(760) 431-6948 (fax) or (800) 650-5115 (fax)
www.hayhouse.com® • www.hayfoundation.org

———

Published in Australia by: Hay House Australia Pty. Ltd.,
18/36 Ralph St., Alexandria NSW 2015
Phone: 612-9669-4299 • *Fax:* 612-9669-4144
www.hayhouse.com.au

Published in the United Kingdom by: Hay House UK, Ltd.,
The Sixth Floor, Watson House, 54 Baker Street, London W1U 7BU
Phone: +44 (0)20 3927 7290 • *Fax:* +44 (0)20 3927 7291
www.hayhouse.co.uk

Published in India by: Hay House Publishers India,
Muskaan Complex, Plot No. 3, B-2, Vasant Kunj, New Delhi 110 070
Phone: 91-11-4176-1620 • *Fax:* 91-11-4176-1630
www.hayhouse.co.in

———

Access New Knowledge.
Anytime. Anywhere.

Learn and evolve at your own pace
with the world's leading experts.

www.hayhouseU.com

Printed in the United States
By Bookmasters